Let Love In

Let Love In

Open Your Heart and Mind to Attract Your Ideal Partner

Debra A. Berndt, CHt

WILEY

John Wiley & Sons, Inc.

Published by John Wiley & Sons, Inc., Hoboken, New Jersey
Published simultaneously in Canada

For general information about our other products and services, please contact our Customer Care Department within the United States at (800) 762-2974, outside the United States at (317) 572-3993 or fax (317) 572-4002.

Wiley also publishes its books in a variety of electronic formats. Some content that appears in print may not be available in electronic books. For more information about Wiley products, visit our web site at www.wiley.com.

Library of Congress Cataloging-in-Publication Data:

Berndt, Debra A.
    Let love in : open your heart and mind to attract your ideal partner / Debra A. Berndt.
      p. cm.
    Includes index.
    ISBN 978-0-470-49749-4 (pbk.)
      1. Dating (Social customs)   2. Love.   3. Man-woman relationships.   4. Single women—Psychology.   I. Title.
   HQ801.B4776   2010
   646.7'7—dc22

2009020803

Printed in the United States of America

10 9 8 7 6 5 4 3 2 1

For Roberto

Contents

Acknowledgments

From the depths of my heart, a generous thank-you to all of my girl-friends who helped me thrive during my single years. You were there for the celebrations, beach and ski trips, dancing until the wee hours, double dates, heartaches, happy hours, football Sundays, and every available man-hunting opportunity we could find. I appreciate the wonderful memories that made my single life something to cherish. To the Jersey girls who lived through my preawakening years, I appreciate that you always seen the best in me even when I couldn't see it myself. My dear Denver friends will always hold a special place in my heart. Colorado is forever my home; a place where I found my spirit, my love, and my calling.

Of course, I must express my thanks to the men I've dated throughout the years, even though I did not always see their gift until much later. With each heartbreak, I opened up to a new level of self-awareness that has made me the woman I am today. Thanks for letting me go so that I could find my true self and my true love.

I owe a debt of gratitude to my teachers. Brenda Simmons, thanks for your amazing insight and for being my rock during my life transitions. A big thank-you to the staff and my fellow students at the Hypnotherapy Academy in Sante Fe, New Mexico, who helped me discover my life's work and experience divine self-love. Also, much thanks to Zoilita Grant of the Colorado Coaching and

Hypnotherapy Institute for giving me the opportunity to teach my work to others. Thanks to all of my clients who have supported me over the years; it has been an honor to see you step into your greatness. Also, much appreciation to Carissa and Heather, my partners at Denver Hypnotherapy and Energy Medicine, who helped create a sacred place for our work.

A huge thanks to my coach, Robin Hoffman. Your guidance and support, both personal and professional, helped me create what I put down on these pages. Thanks also to Shari Cauldron, my writing coach/teacher, who helped me polish my work along with the wonderful group at Lighthouse Writers in Denver.

Thanks to Lilly Ghahremani, my agent at Full Circle Literary, for all of your edits and suggestions and for finding a great publisher to share my message. Thank you for believing in me. It was such a pleasure working with my editor at Wiley, Christel Winkler. You were always approachable and accessible throughout the entire process. Thank you for all of your work on this project and for bringing it to the world.

I also want to send a big thank-you to my family. To my parents, Skip and Gail, you are living proof that lasting, loving relationships are possible. My siblings and their partners, Chuck, Lisa, Pam, Rich, Kim, and Alex, thanks for your friendship and love. My nephew and niece, Ryan and Shayna, you have always been an oasis of unconditional love and smiles. A big hug to my cousin Tom for being my lifelong best friend and confidant, as well as to his partner, David. Thank you both for providing me a home and comfort in one of the biggest transitions of my life. Also, lots of love and hugs to my cousin Ilona, who has been someone I have always looked up to as my big sister. To my grandmother Helen, who taught me that an abundance of love makes you the richest woman in town, and to the rest of the Henderson clan, who continue to carry on her message and faith.

Most important, I would like to thank my partner and love, Roberto, for being my biggest fan. Your words of encouragement and loving support continue to be unwavering. I love you.

Introduction

*Your task is not to seek for love, but merely to seek and find
all the barriers within yourself that you have built against it.*

—Rumi

Do you feel powerless when it comes to dating? Do you wonder
why everyone else seems to have such an easy time finding someone to love, yet you find it so difficult? Have you always been the one
who is seated at the singles' table at weddings? Are you usually set
up with the groom's dorky best friend, all the while being given
advice by your romantically involved friends, who say you are just
too picky? Have you lived with aching loneliness in the very core of
your being and asked yourself what was wrong with you? What if I
told you that you were responsible for creating every dating experience you ever had? At first, you might get angry at me for even

suggesting this. You might wonder why you would choose such a lonely fate. Then maybe you'd realize the good news: if you created it, you can also *change* it.

Allow yourself to be open to the concept that every person who appears in your life does not do so by accident; you attract each one with the magnetic draw of your subconscious mind. Now consider the possibility that you can change your thinking on the deepest level of your mind in order to attract the love of your life. Wouldn't that be amazing?

This book will give you the gift of making your mind receptive to love. You see, love starts within you and flows out into the world (not the other way around). Inside these pages, you will find a very simple and effective system to change your dating destiny. I am talking about permanent shifts in your self-confidence, which will not only attract Mr. Right but also will undoubtedly affect every area of your life.

By reading this book, you are joining many other single women (including me) who have used this remarkable tool to change their inner beliefs and attract their true loves. What if I told you that this technique is no secret and has been around for thousands of years? There is a ton of scientific evidence that this process works. You may have heard about it before, but perhaps you weren't ready to apply it until just this moment. That is why you picked up this book. You are finally prepared to meet the love of your life . . . and he's been waiting for you.

What do I know about love? I know that love is everywhere, and I was always looking for it someplace else. Single into my forties, I devoured every self-help book and dove into every personal-growth workshop I could find. During each step, I discovered a little bit more about why I was still single, and I was eager to practice what I had learned. Yet no matter how much knowledge I acquired, I still could not get my love life right. I kept making the same mistakes, always attracting guys who left me or those who preferred to keep their bachelor status. Nice guys who wanted a commitment also came along, but I rejected them. I worked so hard on myself—why was I still single? Does any of this sound familiar to you?

I knew I had to become more confident in my relationships with men, but how? I felt helpless until I learned about the subconscious mind and how it was responsible for how I viewed myself. You see, all of the dating advice I'd heard previously was simply sitting on the surface of my mind (my conscious mind), without being absorbed by the deeper area of my mind (the subconscious), which influences my life experiences. To see real changes in my dating life, I had to increase my confidence on that deeper level. Once my inner beliefs shifted to more self-acceptance, I began to attract wonderful new circumstances and much nicer guys.

What you "think" is what you will attract into your life. When you believe that you are unlovable, you send out an antilove signal to the world, and ultimately you will attract men who make you feel unlovable. If a man doesn't call you for a few days after a date, do you immediately feel rejected and unlovable? You experience what you are thinking. And here's the most important part: the belief of being unlovable comes *before* the actual experience of being rejected. You thought you were undesirable because he dumped you, but you became attracted to someone who could not love you back because you believed that you were unlovable in the first place. Did you get that? *You* created the rejection. Men aren't always the bad guys!

This book is not about a superficial fix, nor do I include "rules of conduct" to catch a man. You will instead have an opportunity to be transformed from the inside out and change your love destiny forever. The process consists of three easy steps. In the first step, you will learn how to let go of the idea that you are unworthy and unlovable (even if you are not aware of thinking this on a conscious level) so that you can redirect your focus toward new, empowering thoughts. Each chapter includes exercises to help you uncover and let go of negative beliefs and insecurities that have blocked you from giving and receiving love. You will improve your confidence naturally, and

I will help you learn to *really believe* that you are worthy of love. The truth is that you are amazing and full of loving energy. The second step is to vanquish worn-out emotions and behaviors so that you can take action and allow space for true romance. You will also learn about other roadblocks that keep love away and how to overcome them. The last step will teach you how to integrate this new vision of yourself into your daily existence, generate faith, and ultimately attract a happy relationship.

Because we humans are creatures of habit, even as we incorporate new ideas into our lives, the old ways of being and thinking will fight to survive. In other words, changing the conditioned mind takes practice. A lot of the "practice" is described in this book; it consists mainly of written exercises and visualizations.

Follow these guidelines for optimal results:

- Buy a journal to jot down notes as thoughts and insights come up while you read this book. You are in a light trance when you read, so you may experience new insights rising to the surface of your mind with each chapter.

- Spend at least a few days to a week on each chapter to give yourself time to process the internal changes. Remember, there is no rush—you will find the pace that works for you.

- If you wish, you can voice-record the visualizations to play back to yourself. Some people find it easier to do the exercises when they are guided by a voice.

- If you feel stuck on any section, do some automatic writing and journaling about the issue. Freeing the mind and allowing it to fully express itself helps to move you forward.

The main technique you will learn in this book is self-hypnosis. Don't worry—I won't swing a pocket watch and tell you that you are "going deeeeeper." There are many myths about hypnosis. It is a scary word to some people because hypnotism conjures up feelings of being out of control or brainwashed. In truth, hypnosis is simply a type of light relaxation that we experience every day, like watching television. You will experience a trance through visualization, or "daydreaming," with the exercises I demonstrate in this book. This simple process produces incredible results. Hypnosis allows you to relax and let new ideas about love, abundance, and worthiness to sink into the deeper level of your mind. I often call self-hypnosis "training wheels for the mind." Just ten minutes of daily practice can help you become naturally more confident. In a very short time, you will feel more hopeful and lovable and will allow love into your life. Forget about putting on an act; you will become the real deal! Are you ready to get started?

The most extraordinary result of hypnosis is that the mental state can give you a direct experience of unconditional love. This loving energy is always just beneath the surface, readily available to transform you. Most people look outside of themselves for healing when they already have the power to heal within themselves. By doing the work in this book, you will tap into your own loving energy, which can heal any wound. You see, the love is what heals you; it's not me, hypnosis, or any other technique. You were born with your own first-aid kit to patch yourself up after suffering from the bumps and scrapes of life. You are already a powerful healer; I am simply helping you witness your own magnificence.

Using the tools in this book, I reinvented myself from the inside out, turning a frail, insecure, lonely girl into a dynamic, confident, lovable woman. My dating sagas and those of my clients and radio-show listeners have inspired me to write this book about breaking the cycle of heartache and attracting real love so that others can benefit from my journey. There are so many techniques that claim to change your love destiny, and I've tried most of them without results. Adding the key element of hypnosis was what finally worked for me and countless other single women and men in my practice. I only wish I had discovered this powerful method earlier, and it feels so good to bring it to you now.

In these pages, you will hear my story and the stories of people I have helped to find true love.* You will embrace your own experience, comfort the vulnerable little one within you who is seeking solace in a relationship, and make powerful choices in all areas of your life. I will show you how to steer your mind in the right direction so that you not only *attract* the love of your life, but also can *maintain* a wonderful relationship without resorting to the old sabotaging behaviors that kept love away in the past.

Take part in this adventure, and join me in exploring a future that's free of your past limitations. After you complete the simple exercises in this book, nothing will hold you back from attracting the love of your life. Remember that you are already perfect and lovable. There is nothing to fix except the false concepts about love that lie deep in your mind.

Let's get hypnotized.

---

*Note that the names and the details of the stories have been altered to protect the privacy of my clients and radio-show guests. These stories were based on thousands of cases, and any resemblance to a particular person is completely accidental. On the other hand, my stories are all completely accurate.

1

Relationship Assessment

There are only two ways to live your life.
One is as though nothing is a miracle. The other
is as though everything is a miracle.

—Albert Einstein

Before you begin this journey toward attracting the love of your life, spend a moment to take a personal assessment of how you currently work with your mind in a relationship. After completing this book, you will get another opportunity to take this questionnaire to gauge your progress.

Read each statement and rate how it applies to your current belief systems, from "strongly disagree" to "strongly agree." Please be honest; this test is only for you. Don't try to give an answer that will make you look good. This assessment will help you determine whether your core beliefs are currently aligned with your conscious desire to attract "the one." This is the first step toward uncovering which beliefs have held you back from finding love.

Relationship Assessment Questionnaire

Part I: Thoughts

1 = Strongly disagree

2 = Disagree

3 = Neither agree nor disagree

4 = Agree

5 = Strongly agree

1. I know exactly the type of man I am looking for in a life partner. _____
2. I deserve a good partner. _____
3. I love the people in my life unconditionally. _____
4. I am aware of my thoughts and am familiar with the stories I tell myself about my life. _____
5. I easily forgive others when they hurt me. _____
6. I know I am a good catch and deserve a great relationship. _____
7. I know what it feels like to be loved. _____
8. I don't take it personally when men don't call. _____
9. I hold no resentment toward my parents for how they brought me up. _____
10. When I first start dating someone, I see beyond his clothes, job, home, and other external factors. _____

Total: _____

Part II: Action

11. I often put myself in situations where I can meet new people. _____

12. I am relaxed and open when I am on a first date. _____

13. I always surround myself with people who support me and believe in me. _____

14. When I am dating someone in a committed relationship, I am completely faithful to that person. _____

15. I only date men who have the qualities that I am seeking in a mate. _____

16. I express my true feelings and keep boundaries with men. _____

17. When I talk to my friends and family, I never complain about being single. _____

18. If someone tells me that he does not want a commitment, I easily cut that person out of my life. _____

19. I show my true self on dates and never pretend to be like anyone else. _____

20. The men I date know that I am searching for a committed relationship. _____

Total: _____

Part III: Faith

21. I believe that I will meet my true love very soon. _____

22. I can see myself in a happy relationship. _____

23. I take responsibility for my life circumstances. _____

24. I understand how being in a healthy relationship can affect other areas of my life. _____

25. I am grateful for everyone and everything I have in my life right now. _____

26. I take time to enjoy each moment because I know that life is always changing. _____

27. I am happy for my friends when they meet someone special.
    _____

28. I believe there are many men out there who can be my match.
    _____

29. I love the holidays and special occasions, even when I do not
    have a date. _____

30. I accept my life exactly as it is. _____

Total: _____

Okay, now it's time to tally your score. Add up each section to
determine your score for each part. Remember, this isn't a test but
an assessment of where you are right now.

Scoring
Over 40 = high

25–39 = medium

Under 24 = low

With regard to healthy relationships, your score in part I reveals
the clarity of your thoughts, your score in part II reveals your level
of action, and your score in part III reveals your level of faith. You
may discover that your score is higher in one section than in the
others. Keep this information in mind as you go through the exercises in the book. Everyone has a unique combination of scores and
will have different experiences while doing the work in this book.
If you are doing this work in a group or with a friend, avoid comparing your progress with others'. Use this score as a tool to assess
yourself throughout the process. Feel free to come back to this
assessment anytime you'd like to see where you're improving.

Please don't feel bad about having a low score. You wouldn't
need this book if you had a high score, right? To give you an idea
of where I came from, here is my score before I did the work:
thoughts, 16; action, 24; faith, 23. You see, I was taking actions to
meet people and dating many men, but I wasn't focused on what

I was looking for, and I had so many doubts that I would meet the right man. After you read a few chapters, your responses to the statements will change and your score will get higher. As your score improves, you will be closer to finding your mate. Don't overassess yourself and take the test after every chapter. It takes time to adjust the beliefs in your subconscious mind. For best results, simply allow yourself to go through the processes set forth in these chapters and take the assessment again when you are finished with the book. You don't need to have a high score to meet your man.

Regardless of how you score, you are already perfect. You will learn to let go of the false ideas you have accepted through your life that cover up your true magnificence. You don't have to change anything except a warped perception about yourself and relationships that keeps you from attracting love. You don't have to wait until you are "completely finished" to attract your mate. Sometimes a simple shift in perspective can make you the master of your dating destiny.

PART ONE

Unpack Your Baggage and Get Ready for Love!

Relationships are like Rome—difficult to start out,
incredible during the prosperity of the "golden age," and
unbearable during the fall. Then, a new kingdom will
come along and the whole process will repeat itself until
you come across a kingdom like Egypt . . . that thrives,
and continues to flourish. This kingdom will become
your best friend, your soul mate, and your love.

—Helen Keller

If you want to master your love life, you will need to clear your mind of the beliefs that have prevented you from attracting love in the past. The process of self-hypnosis will bring your subconscious mind into harmony with your conscious desire for love. You will come to understand and let go of behavior patterns that have led to unsatis-factory relationships. A big part of this process is learning to forgive others and especially yourself as you embrace your true potential. By clarifying why you want love and becoming familiar with a new definition of love, you will become unstoppable. Once this powerful alignment occurs between your conscious mind and your subconscious mind, all of your relationships will improve.

2

Your Dating Destiny: It's All in Your Mind!

Reality leaves a lot to the imagination.

—John Lennon

A tall, blond, pretty thirty-two-year-old woman came into my office for some relationship work. Her dark-blue business suit accentuated her piercing blue eyes and gave her an appearance of confidence, which vanished when she slumped into the chair. Holding crumpled tissues, she wiped the tears from her face. She could not maintain her composure. Mary had just been dumped again. Tired of rejection after rejection, she asked me whether there was any hope that she would ever find love. Everything else in her life seemed to be going well. She was intelligent and had a high-paying job as a computer programmer. She had many close friends and a great family. But despite having all of the outward signs of a happy life, she couldn't find a man to stick around longer than two months. Each rejection ravaged her self-esteem, and she had nowhere else to turn. She looked at me that day and pleaded, "Can you help?"

After several sessions of hypnotherapy, she learned to laugh at her own mistakes, became more aware of her pattern of selecting certain types of men, and felt empowered to make different choices. She transformed from a wounded victim who felt "not good enough" to a powerful, self-assured woman who really believed she deserved a great relationship. Over a two-month period, her confidence increased through the use of self-hypnosis visualizations. Her life changed dramatically because she was able to break the cycle of attracting unavailable men. Six months after our final session, she called to tell me that she had met the man of her dreams. Two years later, she reported that they were happily married. She strongly believes that her success in building a healthy relationship is due to the work we did together.

Mary is like countless other clients who have come to me over the years to heal their relationship issues. According to the 2000 U.S. Census, more than 95.7 million Americans are single. Sixty-three percent of them have never been married, and many are women. Not all of these people want partners, but a large majority of single women *do* want love and are either afraid to get involved again or do not think that love is possible.

With such an abundance of single people out there, why are so many women—including you—struggling to find a partner? The main underlying reason is because whatever you think and believe about relationships will be manifested in your life and in the people you date. In Mary's case, she felt unwanted and unlovable on a deep level, so she unconsciously attracted men who reinforced that idea. These men always left her, and she continued the destructive cycle of thinking that she was unlovable until she changed her subconscious beliefs.

How You Create Your Life

I believe that certain basic rules exist in the universe, and that from these, everything is created. All of life is attuned to a universal formless substance or energy. Many names exist for this energy, such as God, universal life force, the Great Spirit, the Self, and so on. This powerful force is the common thread that connects all of your life experiences.

This amazing energy remains neutral until it interacts with the thoughts and feelings in your mind. Wherever your mind focuses, you create that reality. This is not a mystical power reserved only for enlightened gurus; you have worked with this force your entire life. Unfortunately, you may be creating situations by default, allowing your mind to replay old tapes from the past so that you remain stuck in habitual relationship patterns and rely on false beliefs about love. To change your dating destiny, all you need to do is adjust the focus of your mind.

Where does your mind focus most of the time? Do you always worry about growing old alone or think that you won't meet the right man in time to have children? Are you clear about your goals for a relationship? *The universe or God does not know the difference between a request and a fear.* You get what you focus on. If you obsess about never having children because your true love has not appeared, this universal force senses your fear and creates that reality, regardless of whether you want it or not. On the other hand, if you focus on your best qualities and feel confident that you will attract a mate soon, the creative force will manifest that reality. You have the power to choose your focus.

Creation Equation

As indicated in Figure 1 on the following page, your core beliefs start the cycle of creation and bring about the experiences you have in life. Your deep beliefs create your thoughts. Your mind is constantly thinking, and you can hear its chatter. This mind-chatter drives your actions (physical and emotional), which result in your creating certain situations in your life. For example, if you have a core belief that

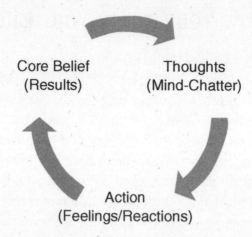

Figure 1. The cycle of creation starts from your core beliefs.

you are not lovable, your thoughts (mind-chatter) will be self-deprecating. As a result, you attract men who mistreat you and rein-force your belief that you cannot be loved. You learn to expect more dating misery and begin the cycle over and over again. Ultimately, you feel helpless and stuck. You cannot find a healthy relationship unless you transform your thinking. The only way to break free of the past is to change your core beliefs, which originally created the heartache.

The Source: Core Beliefs

To effectively change your life, you must change your core beliefs about yourself, which exist deep within your mind. Attempting to refo-cus your thinking without exploring the cause is like cutting off the top of a weed without pulling out the entire root. Your core beliefs are the real reason that you seek unsatisfying relationships, but these beliefs are the most difficult to change because they come from your sub-conscious mind. Many people have a blind spot regarding their false beliefs because these thoughts are not conscious. Self-hypnosis can help you identify and change these subconscious ideas until they are aligned with love. Your mind-chatter and your actions are by-products of your deep beliefs. Figure 2 (see the next page) demonstrates how changing your core beliefs is the key to transforming your dating life.

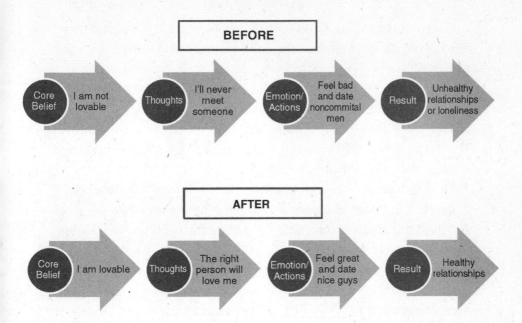

Figure 2. Your core beliefs before and after doing the work in this book, showing the effect on your dating experience.

Your Thoughts Are Fueled by Your Core Beliefs

Gautama Buddha stated, "Our life is shaped by our mind; we become what we think." This idea is said to originate in ancient Hinduism and has been rediscovered in modern times, and there are many instances where the Buddha seems to be right. For example, imagine yourself at a cocktail party carrying a glass of red wine while you are walking across a white carpet. If you think about spilling the wine, you are more likely to make a mess on the host's carpet. Or, if you worry about your finances, you will seek out and discover even more reasons to feel anxious about money. You may have heard that thinking positively is the key, but using affirmations only scrapes the surface when it comes to changing your dating experiences. We process tens of thousands of thoughts each day, and at least 80 percent of them are the same thoughts we had yesterday. So, to be effective in creating the life you want, you need to change your *habitual thoughts*. These consistent thoughts make up your mind-chatter and arise from the core beliefs in your subconscious mind.

Do you ever feel as if you will always be single? No matter how hard you try to find a mate, the conditioned mind brings you back to this same idea—"I will always be single." Your mind might work against you in your quest for romance because of this deep belief that identifies you as "always single." The more you doubt that you can find love, the more doubts you create in your mind. This cycle of negative thinking is almost unstoppable if you do not change your deep-rooted beliefs.

Feeling confident in your relationships with men may have been difficult in the past, like paddling a canoe upstream while the river surges in the opposite direction. Cascading thoughts such as doubts, fears, and insecurities from previous heartaches will keep you down and prevent you from having a positive outlook about finding true love. Your ability to focus on what you want is limited by your false beliefs, needless worries, past resentments, and inconsistent messages that exist on a deep, subconscious level.

Once you restructure your core beliefs about love and relationships, you will automatically think and act differently. The new flow of thoughts (mind-chatter) will support you as if you were floating effortlessly downstream on a river. The struggle will be over as your thoughts become naturally aligned with love. Then the universal life force will interact with your new, supportive thoughts and will help you initiate and maintain healthier relationships with the opposite sex.

How the Subconscious Rules Your Day

There is a clear difference between your conscious mind and your subconscious mind. Your conscious mind sees only the surface of events (the outer reality). Your conscious mind is logical and acts through your rational will and desires, such as wanting a life partner, more money, or better health. But no matter how strong your will appears to be, these stated desires have little power over your deep, subconscious mind. See Figure 3 on the following page for a model of the mind.

Your subconscious mind rarely changes, and any new information you receive typically just sits on the surface of your mind without penetrating deeper. That's why you easily forget all of

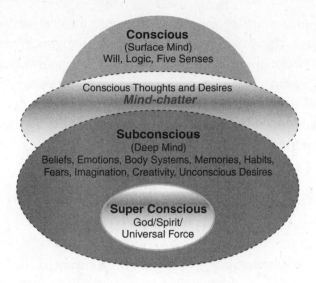

Figure 3. A model of the mind.

the good advice you read in self-help books and instead slip back into your old dating patterns. The subconscious mind controls your emotional responses, as well as your interpretations of people, places, and events. Almost everything you do is managed on autopilot by your subconscious mind; this includes your morning routine, your skills, your bad habits, and your core beliefs.

On the physical level, you do not consciously think about brushing your teeth or driving your car. You chew your food in a similar way during every meal, and you may not even pay attention to the tastes in your mouth. Your heart beats automatically, and you breathe without effort. When you learned to ride a bike, the deepest areas of your mind stored that skill for you to use in the future. The primary goal of your subconscious is to keep you alive and happy. If you try to hold your breath, your subconscious will automatically make you uncomfortable so that you exhale and take in more air.

In addition to all of the physical actions your body performs, the subconscious controls most of your mental activity. Your core beliefs are a part of the pattern that the deep mind likes to sustain. Do you always feel as if you're not good enough or that you are a victim in life? Are you insecure around authority figures or submissive with the opposite sex? That is because you hold these thoughts in your sub-conscious—I am unlovable, I am unwanted, I am not good enough, I am bad, I am wrong, I am a mistake, I am ugly, I am poor, I am stupid, and so on. No matter how illogical these beliefs may be, you are basically locked into accepting them and living by them until you change them at a deeper level.

The Subconscious: The Giant Sponge of Your Childhood

You are probably wondering how all of this unwanted stuff got into your subconscious in the first place. Since your birth (or sometimes even earlier, while you were in the womb), your deeper mind has stored information about what is safe and unsafe, right and wrong, and good and bad, and how you fit into the world. The purpose of the subconscious is to help you function in the future and warn you of danger. For example, you learned that fire is hot and you should avoid touching flames. You learned language so that you could easily read, write, and verbally communicate with oth-ers. This specific information is played back to you whenever you need it. You have a personal database to help you run your life.

The subconscious has filed away your core beliefs just as it has stored the basics for your survival. If a parent, a caregiver, or a teacher ever told you that you were stupid when you were a child, you might have stored that information as if your stupidity was a fact. From that moment on, every time you did something wrong or got a bad grade, the idea was reinforced and made stronger. Even if you received some degree of praise and acknowledgment in your early years, the thoughts that supported your achievements may not have been as powerful as the "I am stupid" belief. Now that you're an adult, this may epitomize how you see yourself in the world, regardless of your external success, because the subconscious stores everything according to its emotional priority. Unfortunately, the subconscious mind gives fear and pain a higher priority than love and joy. That is why we tend to have more negative than positive emotions and thoughts in our daily lives.

Why would you let an "I am stupid" belief remain in your subconscious? Because when you were a young child, your mind had no protection from outer influences, and thus you accepted *as fact* the opinions of others, especially parents, caregivers, and your first teachers. You soaked up every idea, experience, and opinion of the people around you and did not have a discerning mind to disagree with them. You basically agreed with everything anyone ever told you, even the bad stuff. Now give yourself a break and don't beat yourself up for letting these destructive ideas take over your mind. You were only a child. Also, please remember that I do not recommend that you blame your parents for your miserable dating life. Even parents who have the best intentions influence their children's minds in less than desirable ways. The negative ideas in your mind were collected as *you interpreted them*, not necessarily as they were intended or said to you.

When I was young, I believed that my dad did not love me because he did not show me any affection. As an adult, I realized that my father had not been raised to feel comfortable expressing feelings, and his way of showing love was different from my mom's. Yet I stored the belief that I was unlovable by men because of how my dad related to me. As a result, every rejection that I experienced from a man reinforced the idea in my subconscious that I was unlovable. I consciously tried to think differently, but my inner mind still held to the core belief that I was unlovable.

Most of your primary beliefs were stored as a result of intense emotional events in your life. The event itself was neutral until you made up a story or a belief about what happened to you. Often a child suppresses a memory because an event was too painful. As a result, when she grows to adulthood, she does not consciously remember what she made up about herself, even though she now acts on the belief every day. The more suppressed a memory is, the more powerful it becomes subconsciously. This is why women who were sexually abused sometimes do not remember the details, or they keep the bad memories buried deep in their minds, which causes the events to assume even more influence over their lives. By bringing the memories and feelings associated with the abuse to consciousness, a woman can desensitize herself to past events and begin to live fully in the present. This is different from rehashing the story of the event, which simply reinforces the pain. Instead, she is finding a way to heal the wounded child within herself and free herself from that locked-up memory. The idea that she stored as a child can be transformed if she allows the adult mind to see a new perspective. You cannot change a past event, but you can transform your interpretation of it. Your revised story will create a new pattern of thoughts, feelings, and actions. The belief is the starting point that sets a chain reaction of thoughts, actions, and results in your life long after the event is over. Many times what you react to is not the present situation but remnants of an old belief from a previous event. Change the belief and everything else will change accordingly, including your dating life. See Figure 4 below.

As a child, you took things literally and may not have understood the humor in a joke made by one of your parents. Silly childhood

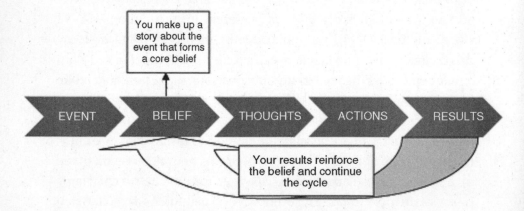

Figure 4. Your core beliefs rule your experience long after an event is over.

nicknames can still have a huge effect on you as an adult, even if you haven't heard the names in decades. You also remember events based on your own unique perspective, which may be completely different from how your relatives recall them. As a child, you were susceptible to criticism and negative thinking because you didn't have the protection of a discerning mind. A filter forms between the ages of seven and eleven, acting as a gatekeeper to the subconscious and locking in everything that was previously absorbed. Do you remember the age when you stopped believing in Santa? New ideas have difficulty penetrating the deeper parts of the mind after that age. This is actually for your own protection; it prevents you from soaking up events like a sponge as you did when you were very young. Unfortunately, some of the older ideas you absorbed back then still lie deep inside your mind and are wreaking havoc on your dating life. You may have sensed this underlying negativity whenever someone paid you a compliment yet you still felt unattractive afterward. No matter what that person said, your mind rejected the compliment because you did not believe the kind words. Your core beliefs reside deep within your subconscious, and they may bear no resemblance to your actual nature. If you want new, lovable thoughts to reach your subconscious mind, it has to be open and receptive enough to allow them in.

The Deep Roots of Your Dating Life

If your subconscious mind holds a belief that you are not good enough, you will unconsciously attract men who seemingly prove that to you. Remember, even though your conscious mind can disagree and believe that you deserve better, your subconscious is in charge. You may be drawn to a man who appears to be nice and kind, but ultimately he might leave you if you still have underlying beliefs that you do not deserve love. The outer confidence that you project is only superficial; your deep insecurities will eventually be revealed in your actions and emotional responses, and this may repel him. Then, when the man rejects you, you will feel the same pain you felt as a child, and this reinforces your feelings that you are "not good enough."

Your deeper mind also interprets your dating life through your false beliefs. Whenever a man does not call you for a few days and you have a deep belief that you are not wanted, you may interpret his not calling as rejection, when, in fact, he simply may have been out of town. Do you then overreact and become clingy? Ultimately, this behavior will drive the man away, which will "prove" to you once again that you are not wanted. This cycle of heartache cannot be broken until you teach the deeper part of your mind that you are desirable and you deserve love.

With all of the nonsense you made up about yourself as a child, you can see why the subconscious mind might put up obstacles against love. Here are some obstructions that my clients have faced:

Mary, the woman mentioned at the beginning of this chapter, had experienced rejection by her father when she was very young. At age thirty-two, however, she was only aware of psychological issues that pertained to her overly critical mother; in contrast, she saw her father as a source of love and support. But after doing a short hypnotic regression focusing on feelings of rejection that she felt from men, she uncovered a memory of an incident that occurred when she was four years old. One day when she had shown her father some artwork she'd made at school, he was too busy to pay attention to her, and she interpreted his dismissal as rejection. Her subconscious stored the experience as a belief that she was not important or lovable. Her mother reinforced those ideas by constantly disparaging Mary during her younger years. This early conditioning ultimately showed up in Mary's dating life because she was highly disapproving of herself. She rarely felt confident with the men she dated, and she blamed herself for every broken romance.

Beth was in her fifties and worked as a secretary in a paper factory. She was overweight, dressed in baggy sweatpants, and felt very uncertain of herself. She told me she had been married three times, and every man she'd had a relationship with was extremely critical of her. In her sessions, we discussed her alcoholic father and the physical and verbal abuse she had endured from him during childhood. She uncovered the deep belief that she was "not good enough." Every man in her life, including her boss at work, treated her as if she was inadequate. I explained that if she changed her story on a deeper level so that she began to believe she *was* good enough, it would build her confidence and would allow new experiences to unfold in her life.

Susan was a petite woman in her forties who worked as a sales representative for a real estate marketing company. She had never been in a long-term relationship. She was lovely and successful, but she kept attracting married men. She had not grown up in a nurturing, affectionate family. There were no hugs, no sharing of feelings, and no closeness during her childhood. When she became an adult, if a man tried to get too close or showed too much affection, she bolted. She discovered that she was more comfortable with a wedge (his wife) between her and her lover, because she had never been taught to be truly intimate. Her relationships were always superficial, like her early family life. The visualization techniques I taught her allowed her to open up her heart to greater intimacy. After a month or two of practice, she met an available, loving single man and formed a healthy relationship.

Women are not the only ones affected by deep insecurities in their relationships. Another client, Joseph, was repeatedly being rejected by the women he dated. Joseph was thirty years old and worked as an insurance agent. He was of average height and good-looking but extremely shy. He revealed to me that whenever he dated a woman for a few weeks, at a certain point in the relationship she would stop returning his calls. He admitted that when he liked a woman, he became very needy and clingy, calling constantly and always wanting to see her. He knew that his behavior repelled women, but he could not stop himself. His neediness took over, and he was always left alone and sad. After a few minutes of talking to me, he revealed that at a young age, he had been taken away from his mother during a divorce. He loved his dad but felt abandoned by his mother. His younger self had stored the subconscious belief "Women leave me and they do not love me." As a result, this idea was reflected in all of his relationships with women. No matter how hard he tried to change, the inner belief was strong enough that he kept finding himself in the same type of dating situation. After a few sessions and the use of self-hypnosis on a daily basis, his confidence increased, he smiled more often, and he became comfortable approaching women. He called me a few months after our last session to tell me that he had finally met a great woman and was really happy.

During your life, you have accumulated many destructive beliefs that decrease your capacity to attract what you really want—a great relationship. Imagine going to a restaurant and changing your mind twenty times when you order. The server will probably bring you something you forgot that you asked for because you were so confused when you placed the order. This is the main reason that your love life is unsatisfactory: you keep sending mixed messages to the creative force, both consciously and subconsciously. Clearing the subconscious mind of old clutter through self-hypnosis is the easiest way to align the deepest levels of your mind with your outward desire to attract the love of your life.

Why Relationships Do Not Last

You have learned about the law of attraction and how it applies to the subconscious mind. Your core beliefs either attract or repel a healthy relationship. But many women have managed to get into relationships with men even when they have a primary belief that they are not lovable. Maybe you look at your women friends and family members, fully aware of their insecurities and psychological issues, and you wonder how they are nevertheless able to attract men. Why do you have to do this work and they don't?

There is another factor involved called the law of transfiguration. This law states that what you believe on the subconscious level is continually communicated to others. So when you date someone, this man can actually read your mind. He may be physically attracted to you at first, but when he spends more time with you, he might suddenly lose interest. You may not have done anything differently. You could have played by the rules and acted cool, but your guy still left you. The reason is that he unconsciously picked up on your core beliefs (which are beneath your conscious awareness), and he started to believe what you believe about yourself. You actually hypnotized him to not love you!

Many short-lived romances end because of this law. Two people "fall in love" superficially, but their relationship is eventually undermined by their hidden beliefs, and one or both of them become repelled by the other. People's deepest insecurities arise when the excitement of the initial passion wears off. If the relationship survives, the reason is often because one or both parties disconnect from their emotions and continue a shallow relationship. Don't assume that all of your couple friends and family members are really happy just because they have a partner. If you want an intimate, healthy relationship, you must address your deep negative beliefs and transform them.

Clearing away subconscious beliefs that hinder you is such a powerful technique. This is because the subconscious mind is not limited by time and space. Whenever you feel attuned to someone, communication occurs on a subconscious level between your mind and that person's, even if you are thousands of miles apart. You each sense the other's deepest beliefs, regardless of physical proximity. This is how a man can sense your presence (or your "essence") from across the room or during a phone call. The good news is that once you clear away the negative beliefs, your love magnet will reach every corner of the planet. When you transform your core beliefs from feeling unworthy to being certain that you are lovable, beautiful, and amazing, you will send that subconscious message to every man you meet. The biggest benefit, however, will be long term because the relationship will last. You will not be "talking a man out of loving you" on the subconscious level anymore. You will develop authentic power and find the love you truly deserve.

You have probably experienced glimpses of the law of transfiguration when you finally got over an old boyfriend and he suddenly reappeared in your life. He stopped feeling that needy pull from you and was now interested in getting you back. Of course, this always occurred when you had no desire left for him. Many relationship books will tell you to act cool and aloof to get a man, but this sham works only temporarily. When you change your core beliefs, you will not have to act. You will naturally feel more attractive, and men will be drawn to you without any effort on your part. You will get to choose from a selection of bachelors and be in control of your dating destiny.

How to Open Your Mind to Let Love In

So how do you change the core beliefs in your subconscious mind? There are many ways that you can easily transform your belief system. The simple answer is to find a method of relaxing your mind so that it can accept new, beneficial information. If you have ever looked in the mirror and said, "I love you," and the voice in your head responded, "Who are you kidding?" then you've experienced the wonderful power of your subconscious mind. The deep levels of your mind will generally reject new ideas that do not match those that are already stored. It's just like pouring water over hard, dry soil;

the water simply runs off the surface. The earth initially rejects the water because the soil has become unreceptive. It takes time and effort for the water to be absorbed until it nourishes the soil.

The subconscious does not like change. Your mind does not like surprises, and it thrives on keeping you in your "comfort zone." You can change over time, though, because eventually, new ideas can sink in. Here are some ways in which the subconscious can be influenced to accept new ideas after your adult filter has formed:

- *Repetition.* If you hear or read something over and over again, you will eventually believe the idea. You have heard the expression "I am going to beat this idea into my head." Quite literally, the subconscious mind weakens its defense against an idea that is mentioned over and over again and finally just accepts it. Have you ever listened to an annoying pop song on the radio and then found yourself singing the tune later in your mind because you heard it so many times? Repetitive advertising, political messages, and the opinions of peers, whether good or bad, can also penetrate your subconscious. Imagine a teenager constantly being teased about her body. As an adult, she may keep the belief that she is overweight long after she has outgrown her baby fat. This could lead to her being insecure about her body and possibly becoming addicted to working out, developing an eating disorder, and/or avoiding intimate contact with men.

- *Authority.* Information received from a doctor, a lawyer, a politician, a boss, a parent, or someone you admire has a good chance of going right into your inner mind. For example, if a doctor tells a patient he will recover quickly, the patient tends to recover at record pace. If the doctor tells the patient he has six months to live and that there is no hope, the patient may die in exactly six months. If a politician says that terrorists are everywhere, plotting our demise, the public tends to be afraid. This phenomenon is seen in cults, where the leader actually "hypnotizes" the followers to believe that his way is best. For hundreds of years, men have taken a position of authority in the world and in marriages. Women tend to look at the men in their lives as authority figures and as greater than them-selves: as people whom they have to win over. If a woman has this viewpoint, then any major rejection from a man, such as a divorce or infidelity, can be devastating, and her deeper mind might begin to believe that she is not worthy or deserving of a loving relationship.

- *An intense emotional event.* Many people find that their core false beliefs originated in significant events in their lives—a death, an accident, or an abusive experience. At any age, a person who undergoes a trauma might experience a radical change in the opinions of the deep mind. While in a state of shock, the subconscious mind cannot rationalize what is going on and relies on emotional responses. A traumatic event makes a strong impression on the subconscious by also creating a hard-wired memory of the event. This old memory triggers the same feelings when it is stimulated by a similar experience. Even if the new incident is only vaguely like the traumatic circum-stances, the deep mind pulls up the old memory and automati-cally replays the emotional response. For example, a person who, either as a child or as an adult, has been verbally or sexu-ally abused by a man may end up believing that "men are not safe." Women with this core belief tend to push the nice guys away and settle for abusive men because their inner minds do not believe it is possible for them to receive love and adoration from a man.

- *Peers.* The people around you teach you what to believe. As you grew up, your friendships had a strong effect on your belief system. Some women had friends who placed a high value on looks, while others focused on excelling in school. Most of my childhood friends were not career oriented, and they became housewives and mothers in their early twenties. When I compared myself to them, I felt like a loser because I was not married at twenty-three. Did you hang around with the wrong crowd? What about the people you surround yourself with now? Think of your girlfriends, coworkers, and family. Do they always tell you that men are jerks, that there are no good men left, or that you will be single forever? Or are you surrounded by happily married couples who encourage you and say that you are wonderful? The people in your environment also affect your beliefs on a subconscious level. Even if you disagree with them, when you spend time with these people, your inner mind eventually loses its defense against their beliefs. You may unconsciously start to mirror their behavior and take on their ideas. For example, if you have friends who are very concerned with finding romance, you may judge yourself poorly if you do not have a boyfriend. If your friends are all freewheeling singles, you may ignore your desire to find a mate and instead engage in wild sexual activities with random men, all the while trying to convince yourself that you are simply having fun.

- *Trance/meditation/hypnosis.* The relaxed mental state of trance or meditation allows the subconscious to be more open to new ideas. You experience a trancelike state every day. The lightest stage is the alpha state. You are in this state when you drive a car or perform a repetitive task. When you are completely engaged and focused—reading a book, watching a movie, or listening to an interesting speaker—you are in the alpha (trance) state.

Think about all of the romantic movies you have seen. Your mind may believe that if your own relationship isn't like those in the movies, you must not be in love. Self-hypnosis involves using simple relaxation and visualization techniques to fill the deeper mind with new, updated ideas of being lovable and worthy so that you can see immediate results in your dating life.

What Hypnosis Is All About

Hypnosis has been used for thousands of years, dating back to the ancient Egyptians. They used the trance state in sleep temples, where they whispered words of healing to the sick, who were then "miraculously" cured. The techniques used four thousand years ago in the temples were considered the earliest known form of hypnotherapy.

Psychotherapy evolved with Dr. Sigmund Freud, who studied hypnosis in France and wrote several articles on hypnotherapy. He used hypnosis in the 1890s until he developed his free-association technique in 1905. After that, he believed that combining psychoanalysis with hypnotic suggestion helped the outcome of treatment. Granted, he did tie all of humankind's neuroses into our wanting to have sex with our fathers or mothers, but that's another issue.

Over the years, hypnosis has been renamed to make the technique sound less mystical and more clinical. Although hypnosis has been the subject of extensive research, and scientific evidence has proved that it works, some professionals prefer to use another term. Certain therapists and coaches have called it "creative visualization" or "guided meditation." Other adjunct therapy systems use the trance state and work directly with the core beliefs in your subconscious, such as emotional freedom technique, eye movement desensitization and reprocessing, neurolinguistic programming, and others. These therapies are essentially based on the same principles— working with the subconscious mind to allow new supportive ideas to be accepted. Hypnosis can also be considered a form of prayer, in which the mind believes and prays for what you intend to create. The bottom line is that whatever you call the technique, the method simply consists of using the trance state to access the deeper mind for transformation. If you have used any of these techniques and they haven't worked as well as you would have liked, you may not have accessed the deep core beliefs that are causing the problems. Through this process, I will help you identify your core beliefs so that you can be free of your dating woes forever.

Debunking the Myths about Hypnosis

Unfortunately for legitimate hypnotherapists, hypnosis has been portrayed in movies and onstage as a catatonic state in which you "black out" or are under the control of a strange old man dangling a pocket watch in front of you. Here are some myths about hypnosis and the real truth about this great tool for exploring and optimizing your mind:

Myths about Hypnosis

- The hypnotist has power over the subject, and the subject is out of control.
- You are asleep or unconscious or you black out during hypnosis.
- You can get stuck in hypnosis.
- You can't remember what happened while under hypnosis.
- You can be forced to do things against your will.
- You cannot move or speak when in a hypnotic trance.
- Hypnotists are creepy.

The Truth about Hypnosis

- You have complete control—all hypnosis is self-hypnosis. You can accept or reject any suggestion in hypnosis.
- Hypnosis is not sleep but an extraordinary state of relaxation.
- You are conscious in a hypnotic trance—you hear everything but are sometimes too relaxed to interact with the outside world.
- You can come out of hypnosis at any time you choose.
- You will never do anything under hypnosis or after hypnosis that is against your moral code of ethics.
- You remember everything during the session, unless the hypnotist makes a suggestion otherwise. (In stage hypnotism, the

hypnotist may throw in a suggestion that the subject will not remember a thing when she opens her eyes. Since the subconscious takes that suggestion literally, the subject forgets what happened. This creates the illusion that the subject was in another world or that the hypnotist has power over her.)

- You can talk, move, and even open your eyes when you are in a trance. You are in a light trance when you watch television or drive a familiar route in your car.

- The hypnotist must gain your trust. You will not get results from someone you think is creepy.

The most important idea to remember is that all hypnosis is self-hypnosis. No one can ever exert hypnotic control over you. The subject puts himself or herself in a trance state, with or without the assistance of a therapist. Just as no one can force you to go to sleep, no one can force you into a trance. Your earliest memory of hypnosis may be when one of your parents read you a bedtime story. The relaxation helped you get into your imaginative mind, relax, and drift off to sleep. The hypnotic trance is the state you are in just before sleep and right before you wake up in the morning. Lingering in that state can be a wonderfully relaxing and profound experience.

Hypnosis is more widely accepted than ever before. The *Wall Street Journal* predicts that hypnotherapy will be one of the top-growing professions of this decade. The American Medical Association and the American Psychological Association both endorse hypnosis as an adjunct to traditional medical treatment and psychotherapy. Famous celebrities have also embraced the power of hypnosis: Matt Damon, Courteney Cox, Martha Stewart, Tiger Woods, Drew Barrymore, Ellen DeGeneres, and others. This amazing resource is now becoming more accepted as a way to easily and rapidly help people overcome past difficulties. The cool thing about hypnosis is that you do not need a PhD to practice it; everyone can use hypnosis.

How Hypnosis Works with Your Mind

The state of hypnosis does not heal anything. Rather, the trance creates a doorway to the subconscious mind, allowing new affirmative ideas to be absorbed. Remember the water-on-the-soil analogy? Imagine that the trance state enables the earth to soften, allowing the water to bring nutrients to the deeper parts of the earth, which will result in the growth of beautiful flowers. As you let loving ideas sink beneath the surface of your mind, you can really start to believe in your wonderful self. As you imagine yourself in a loving relationship, your deeper mind starts to believe that true love is possible, that you are worthy, lovable, and open to love.

Types of Hypnotherapy

There are two types of hypnotherapy. One is suggestion therapy, in which the subject relaxes and allows new ideas to flood the mind. This method is like painting over a wall with a new color. Sometimes you need several coats of paint to cover up the old color. A more advanced method of hypnotherapy, sometimes referred to as "parts therapy" or "regression therapy," helps you to identify and release unwanted beliefs and replace them with supportive ideas. Parts therapy is analogous to stripping the old paint away and putting fresh paint at the base. The advanced method involves more interaction on the part of the subject as he or she works with conflicting beliefs to enable the new ideas to take hold faster. In this book, we use both methods, so that you get optimal opportunities to make rapid changes. The exercises will help you to let go of whatever is holding you back in love, just as if you were having a private hypnotherapy session.

Can Anyone Be Hypnotized?

I hear this question quite often because there are data that suggest that 10 percent of the population is not hypnotizable. Well, the 10 percent mentioned in that statistic are mainly people who have brain damage and/or some form of mental retardation. If you don't fit into those two categories, you should be fine. Actually, the more intelligent you are, the more responsive you are to hypnosis. The trance state is not about weakness but about the ability to focus and harness your mind as a powerful resource in guiding your life.

The Power of Visualization: See It and Then Receive It

Visualizations help flood the mind with new beliefs so that they can become manifest in your outer world. Visualizations are powerful because the mind does not know the difference between what you are imagining and what is happening in the external world. You experience this when you watch television and get tense when the hero is in peril. Your mind (imagination) believes the dangerous situation is real. Your subconscious does not know the difference between fact and fantasy. As you picture yourself in a loving, kind relationship and feel the experience of love on a deep level, the mind thinks you are already in that happy relationship. This technique is called "future pacing." Your thoughts shift, and you draw that situation to you like a magnet. These mental exercises automatically put you into a trance. This state is very easy to access—just like daydreaming. It goes beyond positive thinking, because it engages your feelings as well. Your feelings are deeply interconnected with your thoughts, and your *thoughts and feelings must match* to cause a shift in belief on the deeper level.

With Mary (my client from earlier in this chapter), we used visualizations to create a new story of self-love and acceptance through metaphors and loving feelings. Her inner mind was shifted to include new supportive beliefs that eventually helped her attract her true life partner. She naturally carried herself more confidently, was more selective in the men she was drawn to, and felt more self-assured when on a first date with her future husband. The key here is that these behaviors changed naturally. She didn't play games, act cool, or put on a mask. If you seek true love, you must transform your deep beliefs so that your wonderful inner self can shine through.

What Does Hypnosis Feel Like?

Most people think hypnosis is like anesthesia. They expect to blank out every external sound and lose all memory during the trance. This could not be further from the truth. Hypnosis is similar to the relaxed feeling you get when you watch television or a movie. There are different levels of trance, but the visualizations in this book focus on your getting into a light to medium trance. Deeper states are when you fall asleep. If you find yourself drifting off during the exercises, do them while sitting up so that you can remain alert. You may feel your eyelids twitching, your breath becoming more even and relaxed, and your arms and legs feeling stiff and heavy. Just remember that if you are picturing things in your mind, you are automatically in a trance. You do not need intense training to do self-hypnosis. With practice, you will get better at putting yourself in a trance. Most people hypnotize themselves effectively on the very first attempt. The first word I hear from my clients when they open their eyes after a session is "Wow." In my opinion, hypnosis is the easiest, most enjoyable, and most relaxing way to transform your life.

Hypnosis and the Brain

There are different levels of brain-wave frequencies: beta, alpha, theta, and delta. As you relax, your brain waves slow down and become more organized. As you can see, the trance state is just slightly different than the beta (awake) state, and it is not the same as being asleep.

Beta: awake state

Alpha: mild to light relaxation, altered state, intuition, meditation, daydreaming, hypnosis

Theta: light sleep

Delta: deep sleep

There is still a lot of uncertainty in the scientific community about how these brain waves work and what effect they have on our lives.

Any person who makes an absolute statement about the function of these waves is simply giving his or her opinion, not a scientific theory. According to my experience and that of other hypnotherapists I have studied with, a light state of relaxation is all that is required for hypnotic suggestions to reach the subconscious mind.

There are four levels of trance, each one taking you into a deeper state of relaxation.

1. *Lethargic/light trance.* You are extremely relaxed and may not want to move your body or open your eyes.
2. *Cataleptic/medium trance.* Your body may become rigid or stiff. You see this in stage shows when the subject holds his or her body in one position as directed by the hypnotist. The subject is still mentally alert in this state.
3. *Somnambulistic/deep trance.* You may feel as if you drifted off and do not remember what happened during the session. This particular state is excellent for pain management and can help reduce or eliminate physical pain during surgery or childbirth. Some people hallucinate in this state. You can still be aware of your surroundings in this deep state of trance.
4. *Plenary/Esdaile state.* This is the deepest level of trance. If you are working with a hypnotist, you may not want to respond to him or her. You are in a state of bliss and may not want to leave the experience.

I explain the different depths of trance so that you can learn to recognize them in yourself (and in others). You need to be in only a light trance to experience the benefits of hypnosis. Even in deep states, your mind can be alert and aware of your surroundings. You are the one who determines how deep you go; no one can force you into a dramatic state without your permission.

If you want to go more deeply into a trance, here are some tips:

• *Practice.* A daily practice of self-hypnosis can help you reach deeper states. The more often you enter the state, the easier it becomes. However, take note that no matter how much practice you do, some people naturally go deeper than others based on their personality and other factors.

- *Suggestions*. You can add a direct suggestion in your session, such as "Every time I practice self-hypnosis, I experience deeper and more profound states of relaxation."

- *Repeating*. If you practice with a prerecorded program, you can simply repeat the words in your mind. This gives your mind something to do, and your mind cannot help but let go of the random chatter that keeps you from relaxing.

- *Presence*. Practice being in the moment at different times during the day. As you improve your ability to stay focused, you become more hypnotizable. On the flip side, if you have trouble focusing, practicing hypnosis can help you stay more relaxed and present during the day.

No matter how deeply you are in a trance, you are always in control and can still reject ideas that do not fit your moral code of ethics. This is a safe and natural way to shift your life in a new direction. Transforming old beliefs that lie deep in your mind is the key to changing your experience of life, and the use of hypnosis is a great tool for this purpose. Once you hold beliefs of self-love and acceptance on a deep level, you naturally attract new experiences, including real loving relationships. Are you ready to get started?

Getting Started with Self-Hypnosis

During this process, be aware that your thinking does not stop. Imagine jumping into a rapidly rolling river, and the rough waters strongly pull you in as you struggle to float on the surface to breathe. Most people attempt to get into a hypnotic state that way. They expect to go from having a hectic mind to a calm mind with the snap of a finger (as hypnotists do onstage). Instead, they end up fighting their monkey minds and getting frustrated. They make the excuse that maybe they are not hypnotizable. This is simply not true. Do you expect a baby to go from screaming cries to peaceful sleep in an instant? No. You create the environment for the baby to ease into sleep, with rocking, with soothing talk, or by singing a lullaby. Our minds need to be lulled into relaxation, not shoved into a deep sleep.

To calm the mind initially, you must start with a blank slate. This can be achieved with deep breathing or by simply setting the intention that you are going to do some self-hypnosis. Your thinking will not cease, but it will start to slow down as you focus inward. You will notice your body relaxing as your mind empties itself of repetitive thoughts. Like slowly stepping into a warm pond, inch by inch, you can soothe and prepare your mind for a wonderful hypnotic experience. If you remember this crucial step before you practice hypnosis, you will enjoy greater depths of trance and a deeper feel-good afterglow.

Warm-Up Exercise

Before we get started, I want you to try this quick exercise to get a brief glimpse of how you feel when you are hypnotized. You may find it beneficial to read through the entire exercise before starting it.

Hold both hands out in front of you with your elbows at your sides (as if you are going to type on your computer). Now turn your palms upward and close your eyes. Use the power of your imagination to picture a string of light helium balloons tied to your left thumb. Feel the tug of the balloons as they gently pull your left hand toward the ceiling. Now, while the left hand is going up, imagine that in your right hand you hold a stack of heavy books. Feel the tension in your right hand as the hand struggles to hold up the books. Notice the pressure in your right arm as the arm fights against the weight of the books. Do this for about a minute and come back to this page.

Everyone who does this exercise has a completely different experience, so there is no right or wrong way to do hypnosis. Simply pay attention to what works for you. Answer these questions and see what your answers reveal.

1. Did you see the balloons and/or the books?

    Yes. You have good visual ability, which is great!

    No. You may have been trying too hard, or you may need to work on your visual processing. The more you practice, the better you will visualize. Many times when I tell my clients, "Don't worry about visualizing," they have the most vivid visuals in their sessions. The pressure was off. Keep that in mind. Relax.

2. Did your hands move at all?

    Yes. You are easily hypnotized.

    No. A few things could be happening. You were trying too hard. For some reason, you may have been resisting and didn't want to move your hands, no matter how much you felt like doing so, in order to control the situation. Or, you were not focusing on the items and had too much mind-chatter. I suggest that you try the exercise as many times as you like to get more comfortable with using your imagination.

3. Did you feel a light relaxation when you did this exercise?

    Yes. You can easily enter the trance state.

    No. There are several reasons you might not have felt relaxed during this process. You could have been trying too hard, or you were more relaxed than you realized.

The Reality of the Hypnotic State

Most people are a little disappointed when they first try intentional hypnosis. They expect the trance state to be a wacky, out-of-body experience, but hypnosis can be done with simply a light relaxation.

Some people often experience a trance in their daily lives, thus do not recognize the relaxing sensations in a hypnosis session. They cannot tell the difference between that and their normal state of mind. These people tend to watch a lot of television or movies or read lots of books. This is why I abhor the phrase "going under," because being in a trance is not like going under anesthesia. There is nothing "under" about a trance. A few people can really go deeply into a trance and have more profound experiences, but the average person enters into a light to medium trance when he or she first starts to practice self-hypnosis.

The Law of Reverse Effect

The law of reverse effect states that the harder you try, the more you create the opposite of your intention. Trying too hard negatively affects your results. Let us start with the word "try," shall we? The word "try" implies failure. When you try to do something, you expect to fail. When you try to force yourself into a trance, you are really telling your inner mind that you can't do it. What do you think your result will be in that state of mind? Correct: failure. In a similar fashion, you may have been trying too hard to find a man and then realized how far that tactic has gotten you. So let's make a pact from this moment forward. There is no trying or forcing something to happen. Do you know what the antidote for trying too hard is? Relaxing. That's right, just relax and do the best you can. There is no one checking your pulse or level of trance. You can go at your own pace and have your own unique experience. Everything that you experience will be perfect for you.

Everything Relates Back to You

As you go through the exercises in this book, you may run into some resistance, fear, or other emotions that arise. Everything you experience is directly related to the quality of your subconscious mind and your core issues. Instead of getting frustrated or discouraged, use everything that comes up for your healing. Notice when you do not want to do certain exercises or when you skip over chapters or put the book down before you are finished. Do not quit on yourself. You deserve love, and you will discover that you are an awesome woman as you continue on this path.

How the Subconscious Mind Stores and Retrieves Information

During your hypnotic journey, you will get in touch with your subconscious mind through your five senses. Because your deep mind stores information this way, you can use its filing system to uncover and transform any belief you like. The deep mind stores each belief by using your senses—auditory, visual, kinesthetic (touch), taste, and smell. Everyone stores information differently, and some people use one sense more than others.

When an event occurs in your life, you have an emotional response (joy, fear, etc.), and your subconscious absorbs all of the information surrounding that event and builds a connection, even if it seems random. For example, if a woman's abusive father was always whistling, her subconscious mind will trigger a repulsive feeling when she hears someone whistle. The deep mind associates the whistling with pain. If your dearly loved grandmother always had the smell of baked cookies in her home, you may get a warm, fuzzy feeling every time you smell fresh-baked cookies. This could also be the reason you are addicted to sweets. Your mind is searching for comfort from Grandma, not from the cookies, but it linked the smell of baked goods with good feelings. Every emotion you experience is related to external stimuli recorded by your subconscious. How about a certain musical artist who reminds you of an old love? You may feel an ache every time you hear that singer on the radio. You may feel comfortable in a place that you have never been before because your subconscious is picking up something familiar beyond your conscious awareness. The deep mind detects much more than your conscious mind does.

As you go through the process of hypnosis, you will use your senses to gain access to your core beliefs and then create new memories or associations in your mind so that you achieve a different outcome in your dating life. Each belief that you have is connected to an emotion. Your emotions are the search engine that finds the root beliefs in your subconscious mind.

Through hypnosis, you can create new memories, called "anchors," while in a trance state. In the self-hypnosis exercise on the following page, we will use a key word as an anchor. As you continue with the other exercises, feel free to use the following options for anchoring:

- *Auditory*: You can associate a spoken word, nature sounds, or music with a certain feeling.
- *Visual*: You can see a certain color or image that connects with that feeling.
- *Kinesthetic*: Physical touch—you can put your thumb and forefinger together to create a circle (like an "okay" sign) when you have that feeling.
- *Smell/taste*: You can associate the smell of the beach or rain with an emotion.

In the exercise, you will begin to grasp the power of how your deep mind works, and soon you will be able to create new, joyful emotions at will. Now that you have the practice out of the way and the excuses out of your head for why you can't hypnotize yourself, let's get started with your first hypnosis session.

We begin with the foundation of a "good feeling"—a core state of being that everyone experiences. Most of the time, we are striving to change circumstances in our outer world to arrive at this good feeling. Gaining control over feeling joy at any time can give you a deeper sense of security. Once your mind learns how to be blissful without external stimuli, you start to look inside for peace and serenity. The need to manipulate outer circumstances to make yourself happy diminishes, and you become less needy for a man to give you that feeling. By experiencing positive emotions more often, you attract more circumstances in your world that match that sensation.

Be sure to engage your feelings with every self-hypnosis exercise, and have fun with them. Don't be too hard on yourself and think that you are doing them incorrectly. If you have doubts, simply be aware that your "not good enough" messages are rearing their heads. See them for what they are—old news. Your way will always be the correct way. Your divine mind has amazing intelligence and will always lead you in the right direction. Let's start with this first exercise, which is easy and feels so good! Remember to read through the exercise before entering into trance.

SELF-HYPNOSIS

The "Good Feeling"

Objective: To learn an easy self-hypnosis technique that allows you to enter a safe place in your mind that feels good. A hypnotic technique will also be used to anchor the sensation you generate with a trigger word to use anytime you want the good feeling to come back. This teaches your subconscious mind that feeling good happens on the inside and is not dependent on external circumstances.

Preparation: Find a quiet place where you won't be disturbed. Give yourself at least fifteen minutes so that you don't feel rushed. You can record the instructions on a tape recorder or a digital recorder and play the session back while you do the exercise, if you prefer. Light relaxation music can also help you get your mind into a nice, calm state. Before you start, take a few deep breaths, close your eyes, and clear your mind.

Optional: Before each exercise, you can do this progressive relaxation to get into a deeper state of trance.
If you tend to go into a trance easily, you may want
to skip this part in later chapters. If you have a harder
time relaxing, you will find this step beneficial.

Hypnotic induction: Imagine a warm, relaxing golden
light above your head, and feel that light move onto
your scalp . . . down to your forehead . . . and through
your facial muscles. Allow your jaw to relax, leaving
a space between your upper and lower teeth. Allow
that relaxing energy to move down your shoulders,
releasing all tension, then let it move slowly down
the back of your head and all through your neck. Feel
the rise and fall of your breath as you imagine the
light moving into your chest area, exhale the energy
down into your abdomen, then feel the relaxing light
all throughout your back. Take another deep relaxing
breath and move the light down your arms, past your
elbows, and out through your hands and fingertips.
Take a last deep breath as you feel the light sink into
your hips and pull you deeper into the chair or bed as
the light flows down your legs, past your knees, and
out through your feet and toes. (You can go at the pace
that is right for you and pause at each section of your
body.)

What to Do: Imagine sitting on a park bench in
a beautiful garden. On your lap is a large book. You
see that the cover of the book is marked "[Your
name]'s Life." Open and start browsing through
the book of your life and find a page that reflects a
happy time. Imagine that you are in that moment
again. Fill your mind with all of those good feelings

from that happy moment. Remember all of the details, including the smells, the sounds, the sights—and, most important, bring up those good feelings. Notice where you feel them in your body, and imagine those feelings as a color (any color you like) surrounding you. Feel the vibration of the color and the feelings of happiness inside and around you. As you feel this color and vibration, whisper the word "love" to yourself three times. As you do, feel the energy increase in your body. You are anchoring this feeling in your body and mind in a new way to easily bring that feeling back anytime you need it. When you say "love" in the future, your mind will remember this good feeling and conjure it up inside you. Realize that the feeling comes from inside, within your mind. You can feel love anytime, any-where, simply by mentally stepping into love. Allow this feeling to resonate within you for as long as you can. When you are ready, you can slowly feel your body again and come back to the room.

Note: If you have a hard time thinking of a happy time, try thinking about a family pet or a favorite place. This exercise is an important foundation for the rest of the book and will be referred to as your "good feeling" in future exercises.

If you like, in your journal make a note of your "good feeling" and the time, the place, or the pet you thought about to access that emotion. You will use this sensation throughout the book. This method is called "anchoring" in hypnosis. You simply anchor a feeling with a word, a phrase, a color, or a picture in your mind.

The Hypno-Glow

I coined the term *hypno-glow* because many people experience a wonderful euphoric state for days after a hypnosis session. This feeling is a result of the transition of your mind from the rapid river to the calm warm pond. If you are someone who is always busy and anxious, you may find that this hypno-glow lasts longer and is more profound than in other people who are typically more relaxed. If you don't experience the glow after the first few sessions, don't worry. The more you practice, the more deeply you will go into a trance, and eventually you will feel this amazing energy.

Reinforcing Your Experience

It is important to continue with some reinforcement daily as you go through the chapters to release your blocks to love. When you decide to go to the gym, you know that you can't miraculously achieve a beautiful body in one day (or even in one week). It's the same with your mind. You need to condition your mind just as you do your body to make it feel the way you'd like it to. When you were learning to ride a bike, you probably fell off a few times. You had someone hold the back of the seat until you got your balance, and you cried a lot, thinking you would never learn how to ride. When you were first learning how to ride a bike, the training wheels served as a way to teach your body to balance without falling. Eventually, the training wheels came off, and you were able to ride without assistance. The self-hypnosis process is very similar. Your mind needs to learn a new way to think. So imagine that you are steering yourself in a new direction, I am holding the back of the seat via this book to keep you on track, and the training wheels are the daily practice of self-hypnosis.

The average person needs thirty to sixty days of reinforcement to make a permanent shift in his or her deeper mind. Following are methods you can use to get into a daily practice of self-hypnosis. Choose the ones that are most appealing to you, and perform self-hypnosis every day. Again, you may feel resistance to the new messages at first, but the struggle decreases as your mind starts to accept them.

The Basic Steps to Self-Hypnosis

There are three basic steps to self-hypnosis. The first step is to calm your mind and relax your body so that you can enter into a trance state. The second is to provide suggestions or imagery of what you want the subconscious to learn. The last step is coming out of the trance.

Step 1: Relaxation

Select the relaxation step or combination of steps that works best for you from this list:

- *Progressive relaxation*. See the "Good Feeling" exercise on page 47. This technique is the most popular.
- *Countdown*. State to your subconscious that when you reach the number one, you will be in a deep, relaxed state, and then start counting backward. You can count back from ten to one (or from five to one, if you get relaxed relatively quickly). After each number say, "Deeper relaxed." As you count the numbers, you can visualize them floating in front of you, written on a chalkboard or on floating clouds in a beautiful blue sky.
- *Stairs*. Imagine that you are at the top of a staircase with seven steps. Count backward from seven to one, and as you move down each step say, "Deeper relaxed." Try to feel a sinking sensation as you're imagining walking down the stairs.
- *Hallway*. Imagine walking down a hallway at the end of which is a door you can step through into a peaceful place.
- *Peaceful place*. You may prefer to go to a peaceful place in your mind, such as a mountain meadow, a garden, a beach, or a cool forest.

You are moving your attention away from your busy mind and into a relaxed, peaceful environment. This is the best choice for you if you can become relaxed easily and can visualize effectively.

- *Eye stare*. Stare at a spot on the wall and allow your mind to relax while focusing on that spot. You may find it easier to make the spot high (for example, on the ceiling) so that your eyes roll upward and start to trigger your brain waves into a more relaxed state. Count backward from ten to one and close your eyes slowly until they are completely shut when you reach one. You will notice your body relaxing and sinking deeper into the chair as you do this.

- *Rapid inductions*:

  Key word. In future sessions, you can include a suggestion to use the word "relax" as a trigger to enter into the state of hypnosis. For example, you could say: "Every time I want to return to this deep state of relaxation, all I need to do is say or think the word 'relax,' and I will instantly enter a relaxing hypnotic trance." Then simply say the word "relax" three times as you close your eyes and you will find yourself going deeply into the desired state.

  Quick relax patter. You can use this rapid induction instead of, or in addition to, the previous relaxation methods. Find a comfortable spot, close your eyes, and breathe naturally. Focus on your breathing. Know that you can talk to your body and mind and direct them toward what you desire. Tell your body that it is beginning to relax— "Body, just begin to relax now"—and imagine breathing in clean oxygen and distributing it throughout your entire body. Say, "Body, relax deeper now." Feel your body letting go, and then say, "Relaxing deeper now." Then tell your mind to quiet down: "Mind, you are finding it easier to relax as the body becomes more relaxed." Allow your body to sink deeper and become heavier as you say, "Just relaxing now." Inhale, then on the exhalation, say, "I am completely relaxed."

Of course, you can do a combination of these methods in one session to go into even deeper trance states. For example, you can walk down the steps into a peaceful garden, or do the progressive relaxation, the countdown, and the peaceful place. There is no wrong or right way to do this. You are free to create your own technique. The important thing to remember is that you do not have to go super-deep to get results. A light relaxation is all that you need, so just let go and have fun!

Step 2: Suggestions/Visualization

Once you have entered a relaxed state of mind, your subconscious is open to receiving suggestions. Be sure that you follow this step closely for best results. Here are some examples of suggestions: "I only date men who love and adore me," or "I am beautiful and intelligent, and men love me," or "I love myself." Follow the guidelines on the next page for devising effective suggestions. Remember that your deep mind is not logical and thinks differently from your conscious mind. The subconscious mind takes everything literally, so use great care when formulating your suggestions. A slight misinterpretation by the subconscious can thwart results.

- *Make it believable*. Be sure you make your suggestions believable and attainable.

- *Keep it positive*. Avoid using negative words like "not," "won't," "no," or "don't." Your subconscious mind does not hear the negatives, only the general ideas. So when you say, "I won't date abusive men anymore," the subconscious hears "abusive men" and thinks that is what you want.

- *Stay in the present tense*. Do not say, "I will attract a man who loves me," because the word "will" suggests to your subconscious mind that your love is coming *in the future*, not right now. The subconscious mind thinks only in the present tense, so the idea of a future love never materialises. You have waited long enough; avoid putting off his arrival any longer. Change the suggestion to, "I am attracting a man who loves me right now," or "I am attracting my true love now." Do not mention the past, either.

- *Keep it simple*. Avoid using big words because your subconscious mind has the mentality of a bright nine-year-old.
- *Be specific and accurate*. Use incremental steps, if necessary, and state your goals as accurately as possible.
- *Be realistic*. Avoid using general terms such as "always" and "never."
- *Use action steps*. State the progression of steps you will follow to achieve your goal.
- *Use emotions*. Use emotional words to excite the imagination of your subconscious.
- *Focus on repetition*. Repeat certain main ideas at least three times each during the session.

The number of suggestions you'll want to use depends on you. I recommend that a self-hypnosis session last between ten and fifteen minutes. This is short enough so that you can fit hypnosis programming into your schedule every day. One suggestion said during a trance state holds the power of a thousand affirmations, so think of how much power ten minutes of suggestions will create in your deeper mind. At that rate, shifts in focus will occur very quickly.

You can choose to state your suggestions in the first or second person, whichever feels more comfortable for you. As a hypnotherapist, I always give suggestions to my clients in the second person, such as, "You are becoming more confident every day." When you do hypnosis on your own, without a therapist reading a script, I recommend using the first person: "I am becoming more confident every day." If you record the sessions to play back, you can state the suggestions either way.

Future Pacing

Suggestions can fit into your session in one of three ways. One is to formulate the suggestions first, then visualize the outcome of your intention. If you are reading this book, you will probably want to see yourself in a loving, romantic relationship. Each time you practice self-hypnosis, picture the goal in your mind, experience the good feelings, and hold the belief that your goal is possible. The second way is to state your suggestions after the visualization if you do a clearing exercise with the visualization first. And third, you can sprinkle the suggestions throughout the visualization. Use your judgment to create a flow of elements that works best for you.

Posthypnotic Suggestions

Posthypnotic suggestions are suggestions that are said while you are in a trance, which then create a new reaction from your subconscious when you are in a waking state. These posthypnotic suggestions can be activated on command (just as your good-feeling trigger word can be activated), or they can be responses to external situations, people, or things.

- *Command.* When you experience a good feeling in a trance, you can state to yourself (or in a recording), "Anytime I want to feel this good feeling, all I need to do is say '_____' [insert your key word, feeling, color, etc.], and the feeling will come back."
- *Future experiences.* You can set up a positive expectation for your subconscious in the future by adding some of these examples:

  Every time I go on a date, I automatically feel confident and beautiful.

  Each time I see the color pink, I am reminded of how lovable I am.

  When I am around my mother in the future, I automatically sense her goodwill toward me.

  Each time I hear the sound of "_____," I remember how much I am loved.

  Whenever I feel a cool drink of water hit the back of my throat, I immediately feel relaxed and confident.

Step 3: Count Up to Five

After you have filled your mind with all of those wonderful ideas, you have to formally break the trance by counting up from one to five. On five, open your eyes and say, "Wide awake."

Sample Self-Hypnosis Session

Here is an example of how an entire hypnosis session should flow.

1. Relaxation: progressive relaxation to a peaceful place
2. Suggestions and visualizations:

    I am beautiful.

    I am lovable.

    I am confident.

    I attract nice people into my life.

    I am attracting men who are loyal and romantic.

    I deserve love and respect from men.

    Men love me.

    Men treat me with kindness and respect.

    I attract emotionally available men.

    I believe love is possible for me.

    I am love.

    I have wonderful, unique qualities that someone is looking for right now.

    Future pacing: visualize myself with my true love

    Posthypnotic suggestions

3. Count up to five

You can record your session into a tape recorder or a digital recorder to play back at your leisure. You can also think of just three or four suggestions and repeat them over and over in your mind. As you continue to read this book and do the self-hypnosis and journaling exercises, you may think of more suggestions to add when others seem to have sunk in. You can use self-hypnosis for the rest of your life, fine-tuning positive ideas and constantly upgrading your life's blueprint!

Now that you have a good foundation to work with, get ready for the next chapter, which describes how to release hurt feelings that may be trapping you in your single status. You will continue to condition your mind to create the relationship of your dreams.

To help yourself practice self-hypnosis every day, you can use the free "Attract the Love of Your Life" mp3 program that I professionally recorded. All you need to do is go to www.letloveinbook.com/audiopromo.html and enter the code LLB310 where indicated.

3

Releasing the Beliefs
That Keep You Single

*Love takes off masks that we fear we cannot live
without and know we cannot live within.*

—James Baldwin

Do you realize that every relationship in your life has a common theme? You may keep experiencing the same heartache and disappointments until you become convinced that you are burdened by bad luck. But if you take a look at your previous relationships, you can uncover the core beliefs that have guided your unfulfilling romances, as well as other problematic areas of your life, such as workplace relationships, friendships, and family dynamics. Beyond your conscious understanding, the deep part of your mind could still be holding on to leftover feelings from your childhood that are responsible for your lack of self-confidence and your inability to attract the right person.

In the next few pages, you will uncover this mode of behavior and the beliefs that support your current blueprint for relationships. You need to recognize past patterns so that you can create something different. Your relationship model is a network of ideas, beliefs, and experiences that shape your current dating situation. Until now, your romances may have felt like reruns from an old sitcom, continually replaying the same scenario but with different actors. The only common denominator was the role you played. You will soon learn how to change the channel to reveal a more uplifting and appealing reality. In other words, you will transform your model for relationships so that you can finally experience true love.

Now that you know a little more about how your mind works, roll up your sleeves and get ready to discover whatever beliefs are blocking you from attracting the right mate. Many clients tell me that they have done years of therapy and already know why they are stuck in their destructive relationship patterns. After a session or two, my clients realize that what they originally thought was blocking them turned out to be very different from some of the reasons that were uncovered in their hypnosis sessions. Remember that the subconscious is typically unreasonable. You concocted most of your inner beliefs as a child, so don't be surprised when something completely silly is revealed by this process. If you could have logically figured out your obstacles, you probably wouldn't be stuck.

Unpacking Your Baggage
in Three Easy Steps!

A simple way to uncover hidden beliefs about love is to take an assessment of all the relationships in your life to determine whether there is a common thread. When I did this exercise, I was amazed at the similarities in the quality of my thinking about the different people in my life. Most of the time the pattern is right in front of you, and all it takes is a shift in perception to see what has always been there.

Step 1: Family Connections

Because you started to gather information about relationships early in life, it is important that we begin with your parents. Even if you had a normal childhood and your parents did an excellent job of raising you, do not discount this part of the work. I have worked with women who had a terrible relationship with one parent and a great one with the other, and sometimes the false belief had actually been created by the favored parent. You may believe that you had a great upbringing by both parents, but core beliefs are still created, no matter how wonderfully your parents treated you. Again, the subconscious mind defies logic, so be prepared for surprises.

Open your journal to a clean page, and divide the page into two columns. Label the first column "Liked" and the second column "Didn't Like," and pick one of your parents for this first page. Take a deep breath and let your ideas flow out onto the paper. Write a list of what you liked and didn't like about that parent from the perspective you had as a child. Take as much time as you need and feel free to add more thoughts as you continue through this book. When you are finished with the first parent, switch and use another page for the other parent. If you had more than one parent or caregiver, such as stepparents or grandparents who were involved in your childhood home life, make a separate page for each significant parenting figure. If you had a primary parent who was out of the picture, be sure to include him or her as well. You want to focus on the "idea" of who this person was to you, even if he or she was not physically present due to death or divorce or if you were adopted.

Here's an example of a Liked/Didn't Like list for a mother:

Mom

Liked	Didn't Like
Warm	Worried too much
Loving	Cheated on Dad
Always there for me	Expected too much of me
Sensitive	Critical at times

Step 2: Past Romances

Now that we have the parental patterns documented, let's see what you uncover from your past romantic relationships. Think about your three most significant romantic relationships and make a Liked and Didn't Like list for each of the people you select. You can list specific characteristics of the person, as well as what you liked and didn't like about the relationship in general. Here's an example:

Anthony

Liked	Didn't Like
Handsome	Distant
Funny	Womanizer
Educated	Stressed, overworked
Athletic	Constantly lied
Intelligent	Lived too far away

Step 3: All about You

Now let's focus on *you*. Make a Like and Don't Like list about yourself. Be honest; no one will see the paper except you. You may start to see patterns emerging already. Below is an example of what may be on that list:

Me

Like	Don't Like
Intelligent	Insecure
Healthy	Alone
Financially stable	Depressed
Fun	Needy with men

After you've completed all three steps, look at the lists for similarities. You can get really detailed and write down all of the similar likes and don't likes on another page, or simply review the lists and discover what surfaces. Take a little time and write in your journal some key phrases that appear repeatedly on your lists. This is the model for relationships that you followed unconsciously during your entire life. If you are still not clear, check off the qualities in the list below that most frequently show up in the men you date, and put two check marks if they showed up in the lists you made about your parents or yourself. Two check marks indicate a stronger pattern in your relationship model.

The Men I Date Are

___ Unfaithful

___ Unwilling to commit

___ Addicted (to alcohol, drugs, etc.)

___ Physically abusive

___ Emotionally abusive

___ Poor

___ Fun

___ Happy

___ Sweet

___ Bitter

___ Humorous

___ Juvenile

___ Mature

___ Emotionally unstable

___ Distant emotionally

__ Needy and dependant	__ Affectionate
__ Powerful and demanding	__ Family-oriented
__ Kind and caring	__ Angry
__ Jealous	__ Critical
__ Unpredictable	__ Romantic
__ Selfish	__ Spiritual/religious
__ Depressed	__ Workaholic
__ Handsome	__ Insecure
__ Average looking	__ Healthy and fit
__ Unattractive	__ Overweight
__ Nerdy	__ Physically ill
__ Loving	__ Fearful
__ Overly dependent on their mothers	__ Mentally ill
__ Wealthy	__ Other: _____

Here is what Shayna, a thirty-three-year-old sales assistant, discovered about her choices in men after she went through this process. Shayna wrote that she did not like the fact that her father had spent so much time traveling on business. She received lots of attention from him when he was home, but she was gravely disappointed each time he left for his weekly trips. She discovered that the men she dated always seemed to be unavailable and inconsistent with her, leaving her heartbroken and disappointed, similar to her relationship with her father. In addition, she constantly rejected the guys who were consistent and available.

After reviewing the similarities in all of your lists, you can see how your subconscious has been re-creating the same relationships in your life over and over. These characteristics, even if you disliked them, show up if you focus on them. Your mind has a tendency to focus on what you don't like, instead of on what you do like, in life, in people, and in events. You may even notice that these qualities show up in your friends, your coworkers, and even your boss! Take the top three characteristics and put them in this sentence in your journal: "The men whom I have attracted in the past are _____, _____, and _____ ."

Identifying Your False Beliefs

Now that you have uncovered the general pattern of your relationship model, let's go one step further and discover the false beliefs that you made up about yourself that allow this behavior to continue. Go to a fresh page in your journal, and write along the top one of the following open-ended phrases. Select the one that fits best with your history. Before you start, be clear that this is an uncovering exercise—not an affirmation. We have to identify the exact wording of your belief before we can reverse it. This helps you clearly identify deep beliefs that keep you stuck. Don't panic, we will eventually reverse them!

Choose one of these phrases or feel free to edit them to fit your situation, keeping the bolded copy as indicated.

- **I attract** men who are _____ , _____, and _____, **because I feel I am** _____ .
- **I am attracted** to men who treat me badly **because I feel I am** _____ .
- **I am** alone and single **because I feel I am** _____ .
- **I can never** have a healthy relationship **because I am** _____ .

You may now have a pretty good idea of your current relationship model and some core false beliefs, and you feel ready for an upgrade. You might wonder how you became the way you are or why this happened, but that is not as important as identifying your current model so that you can create a new one. Many factors contributed to the formation of your persona, such as your environment, genetics, and your unique life experiences.

You may want to analyze why you are the way you are, but in my opinion, that process keeps you stuck in the past without changing anything. The task here is to identify what is not working so that you can cultivate something that will support you. I have provided some general categories of relationship models that women tend to fall into, if you need additional help discovering your own. See if any of the following resonates with your experience. Discover your current relationship model and the false beliefs that keep you in that cycle.

Sample Relationship Models

Lonely Lisa is always alone. She wants a relationship but doesn't make any effort to date. She has the inner belief that she is destined to be alone and continues to create the experience of loneliness in her life.

Angry Anna is bitter. She has had many failed relationships and does not think a healthy relationship is possible for her. She believes that she is a failure. She is angry at herself and the world for her predicament.

Heartache Hannah is always searching, hoping, praying, and getting rejected. She keeps going out there and trying again and tends to jump quickly into every relationship. She believes that love is painful.

Doormat Debbie attracts physically or mentally abusive men. She feels as if she deserves what she gets and makes excuses for her abusers. She believes that she is weak.

Carmella Chameleon has no sense of self-identity and conforms to whatever the man of the moment wants her to be. She believes that she is a nobody.

Too-Good Tammy feels like no man is at her level. She is always dissatisfied in her relationships because men do not meet her standards when it comes to attractiveness, financial stability, or intelligence. She believes that no one is good enough for her.

Boardroom Bridget is so caught up in her career that men take a backseat in her life. She thinks a relationship would be nice but rarely has time to socialize. She believes that she is afraid of relationships and that work and success will insulate her from the dangers of intimacy.

Slutty Sarah uses sex to attract men but rarely finds meaningful relationships. She believes that she is not worthy.

Confused Cuthy keeps changing her mind about what type of man she wants to attract. She doesn't really know herself and thinks she will figure herself out when the right one comes along. She believes that she is a nobody.

Adorable Angela is fully confident and always feels attractive and deserving of love. She believes that she is lovable. (If you fit into this category, you probably have no need to read this book.)

Most Prominent False Beliefs

I am alone.

I am nobody.

I am ugly.

I am fat.

I am not worthy.

I am unlovable.

I am stupid.

I am invisible.

I am a failure.

I am weak.

I am bad.

I am wrong.

I am unreliable.

I am not good enough.

I am afraid.

Your unique model and false beliefs may be a combination of any of the aforementioned; reading about them may help you identify your own. You will notice that the ideas that elicit the greatest emotional response are probably your core beliefs. Who are you in relationships? How do you consistently act with a man? Think about how your relationships end. Do they always break off in great drama, with you being abandoned or running away? On the surface, you may not have noticed the pattern, but when you dig deeper you realize there is a familiar tone to all of your dating experiences. This is the model that has not worked for you, and it is now time to break the mold and create a new, healthier dating experience.

It's All in Your Focus

The way you experience life is based on your thoughts and perceptions, whether conscious or unconscious. What I uncovered in hypnotherapy school allowed me to realize that my dating experience could be transformed without much effort. I wrote a healing letter to my dad describing everything I appreciated about him. As I reviewed in my mind all of his good qualities, I realized that I had always focused on what I didn't like about him. If every man I attracted was going to be like my dad, why not focus on his good qualities and experience a healthy relationship with someone who has all of the great things I love about him? I did not need to change my dad, only my *false perception* of him. I wrote that he was honest, funny, responsible, loyal, family focused, sensitive, spiritual, and intelligent. Not a bad list for a potential mate, huh? By changing what your mind focuses on, you will create a new experience in your relationships.

Focus is an important key in your transformation. As I said previously, if you continue to focus on what is wrong, you will keep re-creating the same outcome. From now on, be sure to keep your mind directed toward the idea that true love is coming into your life right now. Martha, a single woman in her forties, consistently thought that she would grow old alone. She focused on the idea of her mother, who had been divorced when Martha was very young and had never remarried. Her mom spent her entire life whining about how men cannot be trusted. After Martha consciously released the idea that she did not need to allow her past (or her mother's past) to affect her future, she started to see herself and the men around her differently. She opened her mind up to receive love and met her mate within three months after she shifted her focus.

You may find that what occurs in your romantic relationships will overflow into your friendships and your family and work relationships. The role you play directly relates to the type of man you are attracted to and want to date. Your relationship experience is *directly* related to your belief system. So in order to change your dating destiny, you need to rework your current relationship model and reverse those false beliefs.

Reworking Your Relationship Model

The process of redesigning your model for relationships can be relatively easy if you are ready for change, ready for real love. You lived according to your model up until this moment, and you are strongly conditioned to maintain that version as your default. Let go of your old self and be willing to try something new; this is crucial in making the shift. You have to consciously decide what kind of relationship you want to have, and then we will use self-hypnosis to retrain your mind to believe in this new idea. You may feel as if you are simply pretending at first and might have a hard time believing these new ideas. Doubt and disbelief are a part of the process, or you already would have found your mate. As you imagine yourself in the arms of your beloved, your inner mind will wonder what the heck is going on, almost like when you are in a bad relationship and your logical mind asks, "Why am I with this loser?" or "Why can't I just say no to this guy?" This positive visualization, however, will be the opposite. You may think, "Can I really find my true love?" or "Can someone love me this much?" Your subconscious mind tries very hard to hold your current model in place. Eventually, you'll start to believe what you are imagining, and then you'll know that the deeper part of your mind is changing.

Setting Your Intention

To become clear on what you want to release, get out your journal and write down everything you are willing to let go of in order to have a healthy relationship.

Examples

I am willing to let go of men who won't commit.

I am willing to let go of making excuses for men when they mistreat me.

I am willing to stop having sex with men until I get to know them better.

I am willing to avoid married men.

Now write down what you want to create in the future, and make sure that you reverse those false beliefs to reflect who you really are.

Examples

I am now attracting men who treat me with respect and who adore me.

I am attracting healthy, loving relationships because I am worthy, beautiful, and deserving of love.

These new ideas may seem a little unbelievable to you at first because you are so conditioned to think the opposite. After a while, these words will be easy to say and believe. Constant reinforcement through self-hypnosis can help your new core beliefs take root.

You'll need to set a clear intention to attract the relationship of your dreams. The description can be one sentence or a few, but not too lengthy. You'll want to be able to remember your goal and have this idea at the forefront of your mind every day. What you write down as your goal is a potential that already exists within you. You are not changing; you are simply letting go of old ideas and stepping into your magnificence. Of course, you can fine-tune your new model as you continue to let go of the old, so this is simply a launching point toward attaining your authentic, beautiful self.

Placing Your Man Order

To help achieve your goal of having a healthy relationship, you should also make a list of the attributes that you seek in a mate. Although this may seem like a repeat of what you just wrote in the previous section, this is slightly more specific. Instead of writing a general statement of what you want, take it to the next level by being really precise as to the type of man you want in your life. This may seem like a mundane exercise, but you can have fun with it. Think of the exercise as your "Man Order." First, go to a fresh page in your journal and brainstorm all of the qualities that you desire in your true love. After you have finished, review what you have written and divide the list into two categories: (1) must-haves, and (2) nice to have. If you want, make a second list divided into these categories and read the "must-haves" section every morning and every night. Categorizing your list will help you get clear on what you absolutely need versus optional qualities that are merely appealing to you.

Just as if you order in a sushi restaurant by checking off your choices, imagine that you have placed an order for your man. By having this information at the forefront of your mind, you'll find it easier to select men because you are clear about what you want. You will quickly weed out the men who don't fit your specifications and will focus on the ones who do. You attract what you focus on. You may be clear about wanting a healthy relationship on the sub-conscious level, but if you are not specific about what you want, the universe will bring any man who fits into that category.

Bringing New Ideas Down to the Deep Mind

Now let's incorporate your new idea of yourself and what you want into your subconscious. You will begin to break through your old model and upgrade to a new experience in love through the power of hypnosis. As we work together, you will find that your hypnotic state becomes deeper and more profound each time. Read through the entire script, then close your eyes and envision the session in your mind. If you like, you can record yourself reading the script with a tape recorder or on a computer. Then play the session back so that you can be guided by your voice. You will receive great benefits any way that you do the session. If you need to go through this exercise more than once, that is totally fine. Some people find that doing it a few times really clears out the old baggage (depending on how much you have!). Other people can read through the exercise and start to visualize as they read. The latter method also works because you are in a trance state when you focus on the subject you are reading about. To achieve a deeper state of relaxation, I suggest that you really relax and close your eyes to completely experience the visualization. There are two inductions suggested on the next page. Feel free to use both methods to get into a deeper state, if you prefer. Remember to read through the exercise at least once before entering into the trance. After the hypnosis process, read the exercise addendum to uncover more about what you experienced in the session. For best results, please do not read the follow-up addendum until you have done the exercise.

SELF-HYPNOSIS

The Wall

Be sure to read through the entire exercise before you start.

Find a comfortable place to relax, and close your eyes. Take a few deep cleansing breaths and let go of all tension.

Induction 1: Begin with a progressive relaxation. Start to focus on your scalp and relax your scalp, moving down into your facial muscles and down the back of your head. Feel the relaxation move into your neck and down through your shoulders. Relax more deeply. Bring relaxing energy into your abdomen and chest and throughout your back. Simply let yourself go ten times deeper as you exhale and move the feeling of relaxation down into your hips. Now move the relaxed feeling down through your legs and out of your feet.

Induction 2 (or "the deepener"): Go deeper as you count backward from ten to one. Picture the numbers in your mind as you count them. When you reach number one, you will be in a perfect state of relaxation. Ten . . . deeper relaxed. . . . Nine . . . deeper relaxed. . . . Eight . . . deeper. . . . Seven . . . deeper relaxed. . . . Six . . . deeper. . . . Five . . . halfway there, going deeper. . . . Four . . . doubling your relaxation. . . . Three . . . deeper relaxed. . . . Two . . . deeper and deeper. . . . One . . . deeper relaxed.

Now imagine that you are in a beautiful mountain setting. The sun is shining just right, there is a warm breeze blowing, and you feel safe and comfortable in this peaceful place. You start to walk down a long mountain trail. Some parts of the path are rocky, while others are smooth. You begin to think about your romantic life and how much you want to meet your life partner but never seem to attract the right one. You notice the trees, the flowers, and other landmarks of your trail and realize that you are seeing the same trees, boulders, and streams over and over again. After a while, you discover that you have been walking in a circle with the same heartaches, the same mistakes, and the same type of man. The journey to love never seems to go anywhere new. But today is different. Today a new trail is forming, and you see a sign that says, "The Real Me." You decide to follow this new trail.

After taking a few steps, you simply stop. You cannot move any farther along your new trail because the path has been blocked by a giant wall. This wall contains all of your conscious and subconscious reasons for repeating your old relationship patterns. Notice how tall the wall is, the thickness of the material it's made of. If you look closely, you can make out words written on the wall, like graffiti, that represent all of your false beliefs that keep you single. Notice what is written. If you gaze down at the cornerstone of the wall, you may see a year etched into the side, indicating the year that this wall first started to form in your belief system. Your inner mind will show you the year. Then take an even closer look; there is a peephole in the wall where you can look through to the other side. On the other side of the wall is the real you in a loving relationship. Notice how happy you are. You are joyous and smiling because this is the real you in the loving partnership you deserve. But you can't reach that new reality because of the wall that was created in your mind, blocking you from this experience. Now, because you created this wall with your mind, you can take it down. So use your imagination and bring forth any materials you'd like to use to knock down the wall. You can use a wrecking ball, a bulldozer, or even a sledgehammer. Take your time removing the wall.

(Pause. If you are recording this session, leave some time for the mental exercise of removing the wall.) When the wall is demolished, continue on. Now imagine unzipping your old self, the model that contained all of your old behaviors and beliefs, and have your real self step out of the old self and into the body of the real you. Notice how much brighter the sun seems to shine on the other side, and when you walk, your feet barely touch the ground. Remember the happiest moment of your life, and take that feeling in. Surround yourself with a beautiful sense of lightness and power. Greeting you on the other side is your true love. Go to him and imagine being in his arms. He is looking into your eyes, holding you and loving you. Allow yourself to get as close as you want to this person and feel all of the good feelings of being adored.

Take as much time as you'd like to stay in this moment and think to yourself the word "peace" three times to anchor the feeling. (If you have trouble attaining the love feeling, keep going back to your "good feeling" from the previous exercise and use it to connect to the idea of a loving relationship.) Spend as much time as you'd like with your love. When you are ready to come back, count up to five, then open your eyes; you will be fully awake.

Suggestions

Feel free to say these to yourself before you count up to five, if you'd like.

I am lovable.

I have the power to attract love in my life.

I believe in myself.

I have faith that all of my romantic dreams are coming true.

I am attracting healthier men in my life.

I love myself.

Each day I am drawing my true love closer to me.

I am a wonderful person who deserves all of the good in life.

Men find me attractive and appealing.

My self-confidence is growing stronger each and every day.

Every time I practice self-hypnosis, I go into deeper states of relaxation.

If I want to experience hypnotic relaxation in the future, all I need to do is say or think the word "relax"; this is my key word to trigger hypnotic relaxation in my body and mind.

Exercise Addendum

If you were not able to take down the wall, keep doing the exercise as you go through the book and you will eventually get there. Some of you may be fearful of resistant or to what is on the other side of the wall and might hold back from taking the barrier down. This setback does not mean you are hopeless. You may just need a little extra tender loving care.

If you were not able to attain the "love" feeling or imagine your true love on the other side, that's okay. Your hypnosis experience is simply letting you know where you are in the process of attracting love. You may have some additional clearing to do as we go through the exercises in the book. Everyone has his or her own pace. Do not judge yourself on where you are in the practice; this is only the first step. Trust that you are doing everything right, and your own pace will be revealed to you.

If the exercise seemed pretty easy, you may have done some other preparatory work to get to the point where you are right now. Good for you! There are plenty of steps left, so don't rush off and leave the rest of this book unread. Make sure that you go through the entire process to get the best results.

If you had trouble visualizing, sometimes your struggle may be caused by trying too hard. Relax more and simply let yourself see what you can see and don't worry about the details. If you continue to struggle, use your feelings instead of your visual capacities.

Imagine the wall inside your body and that you are breaking down the barricade inside your body. Feel your way to that freedom of receiving love. You may find that once you remove the blockage, the visualizations become easier for you, too. The next chapter will help you open up even more to be free from the past.

Always remember to reinforce your experience with your own self-hypnosis process daily. You can refer back to chapter 2 for instructions on how to create your own personal hypnosis session.

4

Forgiveness: Leaving
the Past in the Past

*Out beyond the concepts of right-doing and wrong-doing
there is a field. I will meet you there.*

—Rumi

When I talk with my clients about forgiveness, I am often faced with
resistance. You may confuse forgiveness with letting someone off the
hook. If you carry resentment, you may believe that the offending
person will continue to suffer for his or her mistakes. The reality is
that you are allowing the other person to continue to hurt you even
after the event has passed, as if you are drinking poison while wishing the other person would die. Isn't that lovely? True forgiveness
means letting go of past pain so that *you* can be free to move forward
in your life.

Since you have dredged up the past in previous chapters, you may have uprooted some anger toward your parents, past caregivers, ex-husbands, or ex-boyfriends who have caused you emotional pain. This "stuck" place of resentment can prevent you from finding a healthy relationship. If these feelings are not addressed, you may unconsciously project old hurts onto new potential mates or continue to attract the same abusive behavior in an effort to change the outcome. Once you are free from the past, you will be able to let love in with a clean slate.

Think about the lists of characteristics you made for your parents and past lovers. Does anyone stick out in your mind who brings up strong feelings of anger or resentment? You may think this is the person who is to blame for your heartache or lack of love. Almost everyone has a general idea about which events or people caused the problems and suffering in his or her life. There is always one parent whom you did not get along with or one ex-boyfriend or ex-husband who caused you great emotional pain. Even if you rationalized and let go of your bitterness on a conscious level, your inner mind may not have gotten to that point yet. The process described in this chapter will help clear away any conscious and unconscious resentments so that you can enter into your new loving relationship with an open mind. You don't want those past relationships to continue to haunt you or impede your blissful new love connection. Get out your journal and let's begin the following exercise.

Journaling

Who You're Angry With

Who: Let's start with *who*. Who are you still angry with? If you have a hard time thinking of someone you need to forgive, don't skip over this chapter. Use someone who causes you to experience even a slight degree of agitation. You don't have to feel full-blown rage toward this person to benefit from the exercise. Actually, sometimes a person who merely makes you feel the tiniest bit of tension might provide the most healing. Write his or her name at the top of a fresh page in your journal.

What: Now that you have identified the person in question, write down what he or she did to you that was so terrible. Include all of the dirty details and allow explicit words to flow if you want to.

How: Next, describe how that person's actions affected you and your life.

Why: The last step is to uncover the reasons why that person would want you to experience that suffering or end up with that resulting psychological trauma. For example, "Why did Mom criticize me so much that I never had confidence with men?" or "Why did Dad abuse me so that I am two hundred pounds overweight and I hide out from men?" This is a hard one. Why would they want such an outcome for you? Were they truly evil, or was there another reason?

Although there are people who do hurtful things to others, my experiences in life have convinced me that people are inherently good. They attempt to do their best with whatever resources they have. There are many reasons someone would cause harm to another, such as:

- Mental illness (from mild depression to being criminally insane)
- A history of abuse (from having critical parents to experiencing extreme sexual and physical abuse)
- Being abandoned and/or neglected as a child

- Post-traumatic stress from war, accidents, or witnessing extreme events
- And other unique situations

Remember, the purpose of this exercise is not to let the person off the hook, but instead to help you understand the fuel behind his or her actions. Some parents who were abused in their childhood continue the abuse with their own children because this behavior was a "normal" way of being for them. A person who was abandoned or neglected may not have the capacity to love. See whether you can conjure up a small amount of compassion for what is going on in that person's mind. Everyone has baggage in the deepest part of the mind, and most people are not conscious of it. They usually act on autopilot, based on their previous life experiences, and continue their destructive patterns.

Fortunately, you have this book and the tools within it to change your old mental habits. Someday the person who harmed you may have the insight to change his or her ways, but your happiness does not depend on it.

Freeing the Victim

My next statement won't be easy for you to take, but here it is: you actually helped create the situation in which you were victimized. Your inner mind had to have the qualities of a victim in order to attract the abuser. Just like two puzzle pieces, you both fit together. By holding onto resentment and the victim role, you perpetuate the experience. If you want to be free of past influences, you need to give up being the victim and dissolve your attraction to that type of person. When you release your anger on a deep level, the abusers go away. Either you will not attract them in the first place, or you will refuse to put up with them in your life anymore.

If you are still hesitant about forgiving the past, consider this idea: blaming others for your problems is equal to giving away all of your power. If you allow another person to control your life by blaming him for your dating problems, you will never have the power to change. He may have caused pain in your life in the past, but if you hold on to the victim role, you perpetuate the hurt all on your own. Imagine a man who gets hit with an arrow that was shot by an enemy. Lack of forgiveness is akin to that man pulling out the arrow and continuing to stab himself. Your actions do not affect the aggressor, and you are the one who now brings about your own pain. Even if the other person feels guilty about the action, their pain is not as intense as the feeling you carry.

Since you don't benefit from your anger because the other person is not affected, why can't you simply let it go? One reason is that you may receive a *hidden* benefit from holding the grudge. How does staying resentful serve you? Do you use your bitterness as an excuse to avoid dating, just to prove how broken you are because of this past abuser? If you are having trouble contemplating forgiveness, take a moment to brainstorm in your journal all of the benefits you receive by keeping the ill will. You will be surprised at what surfaces.

Journaling

Letting Go

Take out your journal and find a quiet place to be alone. Take a deep breath, and clear your mind. Write at the top of the page: "Benefits I get from holding on to resentment toward _____." Feel free to write anything that comes to your mind. After reviewing what you wrote, ask yourself whether you can now allow yourself to forgive and be free of this animosity forever. You can do a benefits page for each person whom you would like to forgive and discover different reasons for holding on to the resentment.

Make a conscious decision to release that venom you're holding inside, for your own highest good and for the benefit of everyone.

Forgiveness

Feel free to start with your favorite relaxation step if you'd like to get into a deeper state, but you may decide that you don't need the extra steps. Also, be sure to read through the entire exercise before you start.

Close your eyes and imagine that a certain abusive or troublesome person is standing in front of you. Silently, in your mind, repeat to him or her what you wrote down: "You [describe what he or she did to you], and this is how your actions affected my life [describe how his or her actions affected you]." Then continue with "I understand now why you did what you did because [explain what you think the past influence was that caused his or her actions] and not because you wanted me to [describe the result of his or her actions on your life]." See the person not as the abuser but as a scared child. Visualize how he or she would have felt and looked back then. Send the person love and compassion and let him or her know that you forgive and wish him or her the ability to heal as well. If you feel like doing this, hold the person or shake his or her hand to help reinforce the forgiveness. Now imagine a dark box inside you that holds all of your anger toward this person. This is the emotional block that keeps you stuck in the cycle, and you may find the blockage in the spot on your body where you feel the most tension or uncomfortable sensations. See that box lift up out of your body and dissolve as you let go of old resentments, anger, and other negative emotions that occurred between you and the other person. If you feel compelled to, you can create a beautiful golden cord of connection that signifies a healthy, forgiving relationship with this person.

Count up to five and open your eyes.

Suggestions

Feel free to say these to yourself before you count up to five, if you'd like.

I forgive [person's name] fully and completely.

I release the trauma from this experience now.

Each day I am becoming stronger and stronger.

I am letting go of past hurts to allow new love into my life.

I love myself and accept myself completely.

I am focused on a beautiful, bright future for myself.

I ask my deep mind to clear any remnants of this past trauma right now.

I release and clear any false ideas that I made up about myself as a result of this event.

I focus on all of the good in my life.

I am ready and willing to experience healthy relationships.

So, how did doing the Forgiveness exercise make you feel? Was this a tough session? You can do this exercise over and over with the same person until you feel totally clear of past resentments. Some people need to do the Forgiveness exercise more than once, and that's okay. The process will still work even if you don't feel any love toward the person. The goal is to let go of any resentment and anger that you have in your mind and body. Remember, your subconscious mind doesn't know the difference between what you wish on others and what you wish for yourself. So if you wish bad things to happen to that person, you will have a difficult time attracting good things in your life.

The release of anger is very powerful. As you go through the process with different people in mind, you may notice that some boxes are heavier and uglier than others. Because your deeper mind processes your thoughts literally, simply letting go of the unhealthy energy between you and the other person can bring profound changes in how you relate to that person in the future. Don't underestimate the power of the exercises in this book. The conscious and subconscious areas of your mind process information very differently. Since you are not aware of your subconscious, you may not know what has changed until an experience occurs that proves something has shifted.

Stories of Forgiveness

To help you understand more about the effect of forgiveness, I have included two clients' stories that may amaze you.

Cindy, a twenty-one-year-old college student, came to me because she had some issues with her father. He only spoke to her when it was time to send her money. Her father was very wealthy and highly critical of Cindy. She tried to get his approval but was always met with rejection. Her relationship with her boyfriend was also rocky. In anticipation of his rejection, she usually fired out at him in anger. She realized that she was really angry at her father and wanted to find a way to release the anger so that she could have a normal relationship with her boyfriend.

We did the forgiveness exercise, and she came to the realization that her father had been treated the same way he treated her by her grandfather when growing up and probably did not know any better. She left feeling better but not prepared for what happened next. She gave me a call the following day and told me that I wouldn't believe what had happened. Her father had called her at the exact time of her session with me and left a very loving message on her voice mail. He apologized for being so distant and wanted to meet for dinner. She was amazed. He had never spoken to her with such kindness before that day. She knew without a doubt that the forgiveness exercise had not only exorcised her anger but also had opened the doorway to healing her relationship with her father. She was sure that the beneficial effects would also help her relationship with her boyfriend.

Dina, a forty-year-old financial planner, came to me because of her weight issue and lack of desire to date. She had been sexually abused by her stepfather and believed that her mother had allowed the molestation to happen. She had not spoken to her mother in more than fifteen years, and the rage she experienced when she thought of her childhood needed to be released. At first, Dina refused to do any forgiveness work on her mother. After a few sessions, she discovered that the anger was holding her back with her weight and her romantic life. The day after our forgiveness session she called me in a panic. "Wait until you hear what happened!" she said. "My mother called me this afternoon saying that she did not know why she was calling but that she felt a strong urge to get in touch with me." About a week later, Dina called me again to tell me that she had reconnected with her mother on the phone, and they were planning a reunion. She felt more confident and started to eat healthier foods and work out more frequently. "I now have this loving, kind voice in my head speaking to me and encouraging me to take care of myself. . . . It feels good for a change," she said.

These examples are very typical of the feedback I receive from clients after they have gone through this process. The reason this works is that we are all connected in the deeper levels of our minds. Whenever we make a shift internally, it ripples out to everyone in our environment, even if they are thousands of miles away. Remember the law of transfiguration I explained earlier—your subconscious mind is constantly communicating with others', regardless of time and space. This is quantum physics in action!

| SELF-HYPNOSIS |

Self-Forgiveness

After you have gone through the forgiveness process a few times, you should begin to feel a little lighter and freer. Now you are ready for the next step—working with *yourself*. I want you to think about a time in your life when you were the most disappointed with yourself. Then go through the forgiveness questions again:

1. *Who*: You know the answer to this—*you*
2. *What*: What did you do?
3. *How*: How did the event affect your life?
4. *Why*: Why did you do the act, and did you intend to create the result you experienced?

This is similar to the Forgiveness exercise, but this time you are forgiving yourself. Follow the instructions below and watch for what shows up.

Feel free to start with your favorite relaxation step if you'd like to get into a deeper state, but you may feel that you don't need the extra steps. Also, be sure to read through the entire exercise before you start.

Close your eyes and imagine that you are standing in front of a younger you, at the age of the incident. Silently, in your mind, repeat to your younger self what you wrote down: "You [describe what your younger self did], and this is how your actions affected my life [describe how her actions affected you]." Then continue with "I understand now why you did what you did because [explain what you think the past influence was that caused her actions] and not because you wanted me to [describe the result of her actions on your life]." See yourself as innocent and naive. Visualize how you would have felt and looked back then. Send your younger self love and compassion and let her know that you forgive her and wish her to heal as well. If you feel compelled to, hold her or shake her hand to help reinforce the forgiveness.

Now imagine a beautiful light surrounding your younger self and filling her with all of the knowledge and wisdom you've gained over the years. Watch her grow up before your eyes, whole and healed. Allow any resentment, anger, or other negative emotions to leave you like thick black smoke floating upward and dissolving into the ceiling. Allow your entire self, your younger self and the present-day you, to merge as you are healed and the past influences are forgiven. Now you can move forward in peace.

Count up to five and open your eyes.

Suggestions

Feel free to say these to yourself before you count up to five, if you'd like.

I release and clear any lack of forgiveness that I hold for myself.

I embrace my greatness fully.

I love who I am and the person I am becoming.

I forgive myself fully and completely for anything I have done in the past that I perceived as wrong or bad.

I accept all parts of me.

I have compassion for myself and my past actions.

I trust myself.

I love myself.

I know that who I am is inherently good.

I always think the best of myself and do everything to the best of my ability.

How did the Self-Forgiveness exercise go for you? Were you able to clear out the resentment you held toward yourself? If you recalled more than one event that you regret in your life, you can do the Self-Forgiveness exercise as many times as you desire. Try not to overdo it, though. You could also do one session to cover a common theme, instead of a separate session for each individual event.

Forgiving yourself is probably the hardest thing to do. Believe it or not, most people think they are mad at others when they are really upset with themselves. The feeling is expressed either in outward aggression toward others or through inward self-hate. If you are angry at yourself, how can you attract someone who thinks you are wonderful? Getting to know the real you, who is beautiful, amazing, and inherently good, is a positive step toward attracting the love of your life.

The Benefits of Full Self-Acceptance

As I mention frequently, your essence is already perfect, even when you do things that you may regret. Your actions do not dictate who you are. If you can fully accept yourself with all of your foibles, you can become more compassionate to the people in your life who have made mistakes. By loving every part of yourself, you are less likely to pretend that you are someone else and less dependent on others' approval. When you attract your true love, you will discover that full self-acceptance can create a harmonious relationship free of judgment and blame. When you accept yourself, others will naturally follow your lead.

Reinforcing Your Experience

Continue to do daily self-hypnosis to reinforce your positive suggestions from earlier chapters. You can tweak the suggestions to add on new affirmative beliefs that need to be absorbed as you uncover them. Keep most of your suggestions consistent, because the subconscious mind needs at least thirty days to make a shift.

5

Get How Great You Are!

What I am looking for is not out there; it is in me.

—Helen Keller

If you were turned off by the title of this chapter about greatness, pay attention. People often do not want to consider themselves great because that idea feels too uncomfortable. You may find it easier to accept the idea that you are a good, nice, or kind person . . . but a *great* person? Maybe you feel that this term is reserved for someone who has done so-called great things, like discovering a cure for a deadly disease or climbing Mount Everest. But you don't need to do anything special to become great; your true greatness has always been within you. You simply need to clear away the cobwebs of your false thinking to reveal the true, wonderful you. Still not convinced? You will start to believe it after reading this chapter.

Forward Focus—Full Speed Ahead

This is the point where you begin to shift your mind completely to focus on how great you are. Now you will leave your past behind, tear up those old journal entries from previous chapters if you want to, and focus on the here and now. If something comes up, you can return to the Forgiveness exercise, but now it's time to turn yourself around and face forward on your journey to your true love. Because the conditioned mind is so strong, you will feel as if the journey is an uphill battle for a while. That's okay. You aren't rebuilding something new, but merely letting go of the old to allow your real self to shine through.

You Were Born to Greatness

When you were an infant, you simply accepted (and sometimes demanded with loud wails) nurturing and love from your parents or caregivers. Babies don't think about how they inconvenience their parents in the middle of the night when they wake up crying for a feeding or a diaper change. They don't hold back from expressing their needs and instead resolve to remain hungry and wet until morning. Babies communicate what they want and never question their own worthiness. This is your true nature. Somewhere along the way, you learned that it was not okay to ask for what you need. But when you let go of the false ideas that you have acquired in your life, you will be able to experience your inner magnificence.

You don't need to master new skills or achieve anything to become great because your inner nature has had that quality from the beginning. But your natural state of self-love was distorted over time because of typical parenting and other people who rewarded your "goodness" and punished your "badness." This caused you to lose your natural sense of unconditional love and to internalize the new "rules of love": a conditional love that was doled out to you according to how you behaved. Now that you are making progress in uncovering these past blockages to love, however, you are free to rediscover the beautiful self you came into the world with (which has always been within you). Do I hear a big sigh of relief? The hard work will soon be over, and you will be able to relax into your real self again.

Defining Your Best Self

Gaining access to the greatness within yourself may be quite an interesting change. As you work through the processes in this book, I discuss changing your false core beliefs, but I never say that they are bad or wrong. These beliefs are the source of your life experiences. You can, however, consciously choose different experiences because you have free will. The self-hypnosis techniques in this book do not change your true essence, only the way you express yourself as a person. Deep within the subconscious mind rests a quiet, peaceful energy: the superconscious—your true nature, or divine self.

Beyond all of your core beliefs, the superconscious is unchanging, pure, divine love. No matter what you do, despite the so-called mistakes you've made in the past and will make in the future, your inner brilliance and wisdom will always be intact. You have been conditioned to categorize your actions as good or bad and to try to fix what's wrong. By focusing on what is perceived to be broken, you perpetuate the cycle of judging yourself, and you will never feel complete. There will never be a magical day when you will do everything perfectly. My approach is a little different. What if, from now on, you never categorized anything as good or bad?

You may argue that the one-night stand you had last week or the lies you told your best friend were bad actions. You are the one who labels and judges your actions, however; the judgments of other people don't matter unless you agree with them. Your outward actions are a part of your human behavior, but there is something greater within you. Your inner worth as a person, who you really are, is not based solely on what you do.

Beyond the notion of good and the bad, a quiet stillness exists in you that has been there since the day you were born. The superconscious, in its wisdom, knows so much about life, love, and true joy. You can feel this inner peace and love whenever your mind is empty and your body is calm. At times like these, you feel connected to everyone and everything. Take a moment to think about five peak experiences in your life, and write them in your journal.

SELF-HYPNOSIS

True Self

Be sure to read through the entire exercise before you start.

I want you to pick one of those peak moments you just thought about for this exercise. You can repeat the exercise again with other experiences that you remember, but for now select only one that stands out the most strongly in your mind and seems to have the highest vibrational energy.

Close your eyes and go back to that experience for a few minutes or for as long as you want to stay there if you feel really good. Take in all of the scents, sounds, and feelings of that special time. When you return, write down five adjectives that describe what you experienced. You can use the examples below as an aid.

In that moment, I felt _____.

With those feelings, I can _____.

When I feel that way, I am _____ and _____.

If you'd like, you can anchor that entire experience with another key word by going back to the sensation and saying a word of your choice three times.

As you review your notes, get a sense of who you were in that moment. Were you peaceful, light, free, loved, and blessed? That is who you really are. By stripping away the false self that has created your past heartaches, you can uncover your inner greatness, the calm peace that has no name, no identity, nothing to do and nowhere to go . . . just permission to be.

In this place, there is no judgment of right or wrong, no labeling, and no hierarchy. This is the place where everyone is equal, perfect, and loved. Remember that the past has vanished, and all that you have is this moment. You have a choice of dragging your old baggage along with you through life or lightening your load and stepping into a new way of being.

As this True Self exercise shows, when you begin to see beyond your surface behavior and witness your own inner being, you will also glimpse the true nature of others. Regardless of what someone shows you with his or her actions, that person underneath is just like you—beautiful and amazing. The way people express themselves is a result of their limiting subconscious beliefs, and you should never take the actions of others personally. Try this the next time you are on a date: mentally acknowledge your own inner greatness and also recognize the divine essence in the man you are with. It can make a powerful impact. As you begin to see a man's inner radiance, you give him permission to see the light himself. Regardless of whether he becomes the love of your life, you can use dating as a venue to spread more love in the world.

Discovering Your Strengths

Even though you possess a wonderful inner essence, you still need to align your subconscious mind with this idea through the way you express yourself. You are going to learn how to naturally feel more self-assured out in the dating world. You not only want to feel great, but you'd also like to attract a great guy!

Many single women fix their hair, lose weight, buy expensive designer jeans, and find the right crowd to hang out with to build their self-esteem. These attempts to bolster your sense of self-worth are all external, and just like affirmations, they merely sit on the surface of the old crap. A man who likes you because of your hot friends or your tight jeans is not searching for a wonderful woman to share his life with; he probably wants a trophy girlfriend to help build his self-image. Why would you want a guy like that? The answer is because you probably think so little of your own self.

Whom you attract is a direct result of your belief system. If your thoughts are focused on your strengths, you attract someone who feels just as good about himself as you feel about yourself. The more you naturally increase your self-love, the higher the vibration of love you attract. The thing that makes it difficult to build confidence, however, is the habitual thinking that got you here in the first place: *here* meaning "still single." But now you're ready for a new experience: you will train your mind to focus on your true inner power.

The following exercise will help you discover your innate strengths.

Journaling

Uncovering Your Strengths

Before you answer the following questions, close your eyes for a moment, take a deep breath, and exhale all tension. Allow inspiration to flow directly from that quiet place inside to the pen and paper.

Family and Friends

1. Name three people whom you consider to be close to you.
2. Name three personality traits that each of these people likes about you.

Work

1. Name three areas that you excel in at work.

Spiritually

1. If God or a higher power could assess your three top qualities, what would they be?

Now list your top three qualities and imagine that someone loves you for these characteristics. In the past, you may have read dating tips that advised you to hide some of your nicer traits in order to act cool or aloof. But embracing your own goodness is never a turnoff when you meet the right person.

Most people focus on trying to fix things they don't like about themselves, and they completely ignore all of their best attributes. Your self-confidence will increase more quickly if you concentrate on what comes easily for you and let anything that is not working fall away. If you wish you could be more outgoing, but everyone loves that you are a great listener, allow your listening quality to shine. You can then stop putting yourself down, love yourself for exactly who you are, and express your true essence more fully.

Review your top three qualities and ask yourself the following questions: Do others value certain traits you possess because they get something from you in return for your being that way? Are you genuinely being kind and generous, or do you pretend to embody those qualities to make people like you? Your best qualities come out naturally— if you fake certain characteristics to get a favorable response from someone, you are not being true but manipulative. You can easily disguise a false way of acting with superficially good qualities when, in fact, you are only creating obstacles to loving yourself.

Blocks to Love Disguised as Good Qualities

Everyone loves a sincerely good person. The problem is that sometimes people put on a good front in order to get something. They hide their true feelings, wear a smile, and display what appears to be generosity, when inside they are filled with resentment. These traits may show up in someone who is known to be a giver or a rescuer.

The giver. If people like you because you are giving, make sure that you aren't perverting a normally good quality to the point that you become a doormat. If you give because you are afraid to say no, this behavior is a weakness. If you feel that you have to give something or be a certain way for people to like you, you are not expressing your strengths. Your act of giving is merely overcompensating for something that you believe you lack. Many women express how giving they are in relationships, but when they give while expecting payback or acknowledgment of some type, their actions are selfish. They give to get. This is not true benevolence.

Check to see what your past expectations have been in regard to your generosity. Have you felt bitter or resentful because you gave so much to someone and got nothing (not even a thank-you) in return? Do you feel really disappointed if you give something and your gift is not appreciated? Do you feel as if people always take from you and you have a difficult time setting boundaries with them? If you answered yes to any of these questions, your generosity has an unhealthy or neurotic aspect.

Example. Mary from chapter 1 listed her father, her sister, and her best friend as the people she was closest to. They all liked that she was funny, sensitive, and giving. At work, she felt that her best qualities were her intelligence, organization, and dependability. Spiritually, she wrote that God would think she was loyal, lighthearted, and loving. The men she dated were often unable to commit. Whenever a man left her, Mary tried to use her giving personality to manipulate him to come back. She always gave too much to the wrong guys, who did not appreciate her. After experiencing a few heartbreaks, she began to resent her giving nature and saw her generosity as a weakness. The problem was not in the giving, however, but in *why* she gave. When she became more self-confident, she attracted nicer men who did not take advantage of her generosity. She let go of the need to give to get, and she gave only when she felt inclined to do so, without expecting anything in return. She finally attracted a wonderful man who loved her unconditionally and who shared her same giving nature. When she really began to love who she was and allowed her true self to shine, she was able to experience the give-and-take of a healthy relationship.

The rescuer. More intense than the giver, the rescuer is always finding people who need help. She gets her satisfaction from lifting others up out of their miserable existence. It sounds very honorable, but what this savior is actually doing is avoiding her own problems. The rescuer finds poor, unfortunate souls who are addicts, unemployed, emotionally unstable, and so on. Get the picture? She believes that if she rescues a man like this, she will be worthy of being loved—or maybe even adored because the man is so grateful to his "saving angel."

Unfortunately, most wounded people whom she tries to rescue do not appreciate her or, worse, continue to have problems. Then the rescuer feels as if she is a failure, and she sticks around a little longer (sometimes for decades) until the man she thinks she loves finds his way. If he becomes better, she finds another injured bird to heal.

If you are a rescuer, you probably learned this behavior when you were a child. If you witnessed your mother always being the one to bail your family members out of jail or their financial crises, you may have been unconsciously trained to do the same. Or, you could have learned to rescue by taking care of your siblings or your alcoholic father. The rescuer feels as if she always needs someone to save in order to be worthy of love.

Example. Leslie was a fifty-five-year-old salon owner. Her mother had been bedridden when Leslie was very young, so she was in charge of taking care of her mother and her three younger siblings. Nothing Leslie did was ever good enough, though, and her father took out all of his frustrations on her. She felt that if she worked hard at taking care of everyone, he wouldn't yell at her so much.

When Leslie became an adult, she was only happy when she had someone to help. Her boyfriends had all been alcoholics, unemployed, depressed, or physically ill. She also attracted clients, coworkers, and friends who had lots of personal problems. She read all of the latest self-help books and was ready to share her wise advice with anyone who was willing to listen. Her self-worth depended on her helping others, and her salon was the perfect place for her to fulfill her destiny. After years of frustrating relationships, she turned to me for help. She had always been proud of her saving nature until she realized that it was simply a way to ignore her own issues. I explained to her that rescuers believe that love is outside of them, that they have to do something in order to feel worthy. Her rescuing activities only worked superficially in her attempt to fix the deeper issue of her low self-esteem. When she viewed a man as someone who needed to be saved, it was an artificial way to make her feel better than him. By changing her beliefs on a deep level—transforming her core belief of feeling unworthy into an awareness of her divine inner self—she was able to naturally help in the world without using her actions to build herself up. She ultimately attracted someone who did not need to be saved and who loved her unconditionally. She was able to receive without the internal pressure of returning the favor.

If you think you have giver or rescuer issues, you can heal them by identifying the core beliefs around your behavior. Refer back to the list of core beliefs in chapter 3. These ideas are at the root of why you want to please and help people beyond what is normally expected. The second step is to reverse the beliefs to make them affirmative, and be sure to use self-hypnosis suggestions such as these:

I am whole and complete.

I have value.

I give to myself first and then I can give to others.

I am responsible only for myself.

Review your list of top strengths, and make sure your words come from that pure and authentic place within yourself. If you have listed any giver or rescuer traits, try to come up with other values that are more empowering. You have so many wonderful qualities, I am sure you can find some good ones for your top three.

Building Strength in the Inner Mind

Now let's make sure that all of the wonderful strengths you discovered about yourself will be absorbed and recognized at the subconscious level. For this exercise, you will first release more of the false thoughts and clear the way for new ideas. This is a very simple hypnosis technique that you can do even while you are performing everyday tasks. To make the initial exercise more effective, you will first get into a nice trance state.

SELF-HYPNOSIS

The Blackboard

Be sure to read through the entire exercise before you start.

Find a peaceful place where you will not be disturbed. Close your eyes and take a few deep breaths. Clear your mind and turn inward. Notice the rise and fall of your breath. Forget about all of the past exercises, and just be in the here and now.

Imagine that a large blackboard is hanging one to two feet in front of you. You are holding red chalk in your weaker, nondominant hand, ready to write. First, think about your single status. Allow any negative ideas—thoughts that do not support you—to arise in your mind, and write them all on the chalkboard. Keep writing with your weaker hand until your mind is completely emptied of those false beliefs. Stop for a moment and acknowledge how the power of these thoughts has created your dating experience up until now. Act as if you are speaking directly to them and tell them they are no longer valid. They must go now. Take a big eraser and start erasing those false beliefs until you see only the blank blackboard. You may see some red chalk words resurface, fighting for survival, but keep erasing them until they are all gone.

Now imagine a special peak moment in your life, allow those good feelings to flow, and, using white chalk in your dominant hand, start to write all of your strengths on the board. When false thoughts pop up in red on the blackboard again, you can easily erase them, but the strengths written in white chalk cannot be rubbed away. The reason the white cannot be erased is because those ideas are your truths. The truth of who you are cannot be altered, erased, or mutated. The red chalk ideas are temporary, have no value, and are not real. The red ideas were written with your weak hand; they have no power over you.

Now, looking at those wonderful qualities in white, imagine the words moving closer to fill you as they are suffused in a beautiful white light. This light comes from your true divine essence. Feel the words' vibration as clean, powerful, and loving while they move inside you. Let your entire body be immersed in the white light of your truth. Think or say your "good feeling" word three times to anchor that feeling.

Hold that feeling and imagine traveling into the future and seeing yourself in a loving, healthy relationship with a man who adores all of your wonderful qualities. Feel yourself acknowledged, loved, and free.

Embrace your own powerful greatness. You are amazing, brilliant, and wonderful (feel free to insert your own strengths here). You deserve love, you are worthy of a healthy relationship, you are loved and are always safe and secure.

You can take this feeling back with you even after the session is over.

In a moment, count up to five and come back to the present, fully aware and feeling great. (A special note to those who are ambidextrous: do not worry about dominant and weak hands. The process will still work.)

Do you feel more empowered now? Did you notice how, after a while, the red words dissolved on their own? Take note of any red phrases or words that kept resurfacing. Repetitive ideas have a strong hold on you and need more redirecting. If you felt that some words were resistant to being erased or kept resurfacing during the Blackboard exercise, the following journaling activity will help shift them.

Journaling

Reversing Negative Thoughts

Open your journal to a blank page and write on the left-hand side any negative words or phrases that kept creeping up. On the right, reverse those thoughts into more supportive ideas.

For example, "I am not lovable" turns into "I am lovable." "I am ugly" turns into "I am beautiful." "I am fat" turns into "I love my body."

Write your new ideas on a piece of paper and place it somewhere that you look several times each day, such as on your bathroom or bedroom mirror, on your car's dashboard, or even tucked into your wallet. Since your mind is naturally in a trance most of the day, the subconscious absorbs ideas that it repeatedly sees, just like a commercial that you see and hear over and over again.

Return to the Blackboard exercise after a week, and notice how much more easily you can dissolve the old ideas written in red chalk and write down the white supportive beliefs that stick. This may take longer than a week, but you will eventually see a shift as you continue the other exercises in this book.

When you feel good about yourself, your perception of reality is colored by this feeling, almost as if you are wearing "rose-colored glasses." Yes, you'll still experience the normal vicissitudes of life, but with an inner strength and equanimity to help you through any crisis that comes your way. When you *really believe* that you are worthy of having a good man in your life, you will project that confidence out into the world to draw him to you. Honing your attractor magnet is simply a matter of focus. Be aware of where you direct your mind; you can be in charge of your dating experiences. Wherever your mind goes, the energy flows. Focus on your wonderful self, and she will undoubtedly shine through.

Reinforcing Your Experience

Continue with your daily self-hypnosis exercise. Incorporate any new suggestions into it that you feel would benefit you. Use the previous exercise to keep track of how your mind is refocusing on your good qualities. Also, keep your top three best qualities in mind when you are on a date or at a social event. Don't be afraid to give yourself a pat on the back and a confidence boost.

If you'd like, pick up a bead bracelet at a local novelty store or a metaphysical store. Whenever you get the urge to, hold each bead and say one main affirmation over each one until you have gone through all of the beads in the bracelet. You don't have to say them out loud if you are in a public place. You can combine a few affirmations on each bead if you like. The affirmations are a great way to remind yourself how wonderful you are in between your self-hypnosis activities.

6

Being Clear on Why You Want Love

You are what your deep, driving desire is.
As your desire is, so is your will.
As your will is, so is your deed.
As your deed is, so is your destiny.

—Brihadaranyaka, *The Upanishads*

Do you know why you picked up this book? Why do you want a
relationship . . . really? Often you may want something but don't
know the true reasons for your desire. Do you want a man in your
life so that you can avoid being alone or to be a part of the couples'
crowd? Or do you want a partner in order to fit into society, because
you believe that being single is not normal? Maybe it's because you
want to get married and have children. Are you trying to escape your

loneliness or get over the previous guy? If you set the intention to find love and are not clear on what you want to create, you may end up attracting someone who is not right for you . . . again. To understand why you want love, you must grasp the mechanics of the law of attraction and determine where the seeds of desire are buried.

Uncovering the Source of Desire

Although I discussed the basics of how our minds work, and you understand the power of your subconscious mind, I will go one step further. We have superficial desires and deep desires. The surface desires are those we are aware of consciously. They seem logical and reasonable to us. Yet the source of those desires, deep in your inner mind, may be deceptively different from what you believe your intention to be.

These deep desires are closely related to your core beliefs. If you have a core belief that you are not wanted, your deep desire is to be wanted. This deeper craving may be the reason you are searching for a mate—to quench the craving to feel wanted. Unfortunately, no man who comes into your life could ever satisfy that need.

Our desires have many layers, just like an onion. For example, the outer layer contains a yearning for a loving partner similar to the thin skin that crumples off easily. Underneath the surface, there are deeper aspects that you may not be conscious of. To be fully satisfied, you must take care of the real unmet needs instead of the surface wants. The superficial yearnings always look for a quick fix, but if you settle for this, your deeper needs are never satisfied.

To effectively use your mind to attract your true love, you must discover the real reason for the desire. If you don't, you will always be fixing the outer layer of your life and never feel a sense of inner peace. The deep desires are the foundation of all of your efforts in dating. If you heed your superficial yearnings, you are patching up your heartaches with duct tape, but you never heal the root cause of the problem. To ensure that you correct your course, you need to define and satisfy your true longing. Once you fulfill the deeper need, you can watch your love life shift and naturally flow from there. You then approach dating as a creative act; you will desire a loving relationship to add to your life experiences, instead of to fix what you perceive to be broken.

Patty, a thirty-five-year-old insurance executive, always had a man in her life but never anyone who would commit to her. The men always seemed unready for a serious relationship or they got cold feet when she asked them to take their partnership to the next level. Patty was an intelligent, beautiful woman, and her friends could not believe she was still single. Confident and self-aware, she couldn't figure out what she was doing wrong. She came to me hoping that I could help her discover the reason for her dysfunctional love life. During our sessions, she realized that her true, deep desire was not to be alone. On the surface, she believed that a man would fix the ache of lonesomeness. Her deepest longing was not to find a man, but to avoid feeling alone. Patty healed her loneliness through hypnosis and became comfortable in her own skin, whether or not she was with a man. Once she resolved her real issue, she attracted more committed men into her life. She was also able to relax around men because she knew that they were not responsible for satisfying her needs. Fulfilling your own desires helps you become more confident and attractive to men. Avoid falling into the trap of looking outside; the answers are always within you.

True and False Desires

Life isn't all about having things or finding your soul mate, as many other "law of attraction experts" profess. Other people or external things can never really make you happy. Surface desires drive you toward temporary solutions, which result in your always needing more. Uncovering and satisfying your true, deep desires will lead you down a path of lasting joy and inner peace.

Even though humans have a different level of consciousness than animals do, people can still act like sheep. They follow what others are doing, without questioning themselves. Getting caught up in the race of life, they fall into patterns of living that mirror those around them. Society, the media, and family members can put enormous pressure on an individual to find a partner. Brainwashed into thinking that you are nothing without a man, you may get so consumed by the craving for a mate that you forget why you wanted him in the first place. These false desires keep you stuck in a state of suffering. Assuaging longings like this can never truly make you happy or satisfy you. It's similar to eating a great meal: eventually, the food digests and you have to feed yourself again. False desires are temporary.

In Buddhism, there is a spirit being called a "hungry ghost." It was described to me as a creature with a very large stomach, a long, skinny neck, and an extremely small mouth, barely the size of a pinhole. The hungry ghosts can never get enough to curb their hunger. The concept of a hungry ghost can also be used metaphorically, to indicate a psychological state in human beings. A person with this mentality would have an immense, voracious craving for something but, no matter how much he or she consumed, could never be never satisfied. You witness this in the world with the craving for money, fame, personal achievement, and lasting love. No matter how good your life seems to be, you will always want more if your happiness is conditioned on a false or surface desire.

You can recognize a false desire when you find yourself becoming attached to external things, such as other people, finances, or various material items. If you long to get married so that you can impress others with your handsome catch, flash a large diamond engagement ring, or have a lavish wedding, these would be considered superficial conscious desires. Jessica, a twenty-five-year-old mortgage broker, told me that one main reason she wanted to get married was to gain her parents' approval. Silvia, a forty-five-year-old single photographer, told me that she discovered that underneath her desire for a mate was a need for financial stability. After supporting herself financially during her entire adult life, she was ready for a man to come and rescue her with his steady job. Even if she did meet

Mr. Financially Right, however, he could never fully satisfy her because she does not really want money but something deeper. The house, the fancy car, and the furniture provide only a false sense of security. They will eventually get old and need to be replaced, and the hungry ghost inside her mind will salivate for newer, different, and better things. The justifications for needing a man can come in any of these forms, but they are usually driven by deeper desires that lie beneath the conscious mind.

You can recognize your true desires because they are feeling-based. Beyond what you superficially think you want, an emotional need drives that desire and can only be satisfied internally. For most of my clients, the desire for a relationship is based on wanting to feel loved and accepted as a result of unmet needs from childhood. But if you want a mate as a cure for your lack of self-love, the result can be another unhealthy relationship. Consequently, any man you date will pick up your vibe of neediness and leave you either immediately or after the initial physical attraction wears off.

If you always jump into a relationship too quickly and then watch the romance fizzle out just as rapidly, this could be the reason why. There is nothing wrong with wanting to be in a relationship, of course. But you must let go of the *unhealthy* desires and expectations that typically reside in the subconscious before a truly loving partnership can emerge in your life.

Journaling

Free-Form Writing

This exercise will help you uncover the desires that are both on the surface and underneath your awareness. Take out your journal and clear your mind with a cleansing deep breath. On a blank sheet, write at the top: "If I had a loving relationship, how would my life be different?" Take as much time as you need to freely write everything that comes to your mind (even if you think it sounds ridiculous) until you cannot come up with any more ideas.

Now review what you have written. Notice which idea came up the strongest and which ideas were surface-level (I would have a house or children) as compared to inner, emotional desires that were feeling-based (I would feel joy, acceptance, and love). Mark an "S" next to the surface desires and a "D" next to the inner, deep desires.

Journaling

Taking Your Desires to the Next Level

Take all of your surface desires and identify a "feeling" word that represents how you would feel if you attained that goal. For example,

If I had children, I would feel _____ .

If I had a companion, I would feel _____ .

If I had a home, I would feel _____ .

When you are done, notice the pattern of feeling words. The words may be different, but they most likely have a thread of similarity.

Why Do You *Really* Want a Man?

What is your deepest desire? Do you want to feel loved, accepted, or connected? You see, like the quote at the beginning of this chapter from *The Upanishads*, your deepest desire will drive your destiny. Unfortunately, what you may have experienced up until now is the opposite of what you think your desire is. This gets a little wacky, so bear with me. The word "desire" in this case is the energy you are currently emulating. If you have the need to be loved, your energy holds "need," not "being loved." So, according to the law of attraction, you continue to attract the *need* to be loved with your failed romantic pursuits. If you hold a core belief that you are not loved, you set off a chain reaction in your creation equation to manifest that reality. To turn the yearning around, you must fulfill the unmet need within yourself first, and then your deepest desire (or the energy you emulate) becomes "feeling loved" and is ultimately your destiny.

Feel—Act—Receive

You have been programmed to do something in order to have something, such as the feeling you want. For example, if you act the right way, you will get a man and then you'll be happy. Because you were trained to start with the *doing* aspect of this equation, you become tied to the action (the external) to reach your goals. But ultimately, what you really want is the end result—the feeling.

Act	Receive	Feel
Follow the "rules"	A man	Happy

In order to use the law of attraction successfully, you must discover your true inner desire and *fulfill that need on your own*, and then you will always attract what you want.

Feel	Act	Receive
Happy	As natural self	True love

If you start by simply feeling the end result, no matter what happens externally, you will always be in control of your emotions. This is much more satisfying than giving away your power, waiting for someone outside of yourself to come along and tell you that you are worthy, sweep you off your feet, and make you happy. To switch your desire to be aligned with attracting true love, you must find ways to be joyful without a man. I am not asking you to give up the search, but to refrain from being so dependent on a man to deliver happiness to you.

Deepest Desires

Take out your journal and open it to a blank page. Ask yourself this question: "If my deepest desire is to feel_____ , what would a man do to fulfill that?" Then list all of the things you would want a man to do.

Example: If my deepest desire is to feel *loved*, how would a man make me feel *loved*?

Showing physical affection

Calling me

Sending me love notes or e-mails

Telling me that he loves me

Taking me out for special occasions

Review the list you just made, and select the things that you can do right now without a man to have the experience of feeling [insert your deepest desire]. Then come up with some other things that you can do without a man. List them all in your journal.

Here's an example of how this journaling exercise helped a client of mine. Kelly wanted to feel accepted and loved, and she was waiting for a man to make her feel that way. She discovered while doing this exercise that she feels accepted and loved when she volunteers at a local animal shelter walking the dogs. She had never noticed how much that activity helped her before because she was so focused on finding Mr. Right. I encouraged her to be aware of the acceptance and love she felt during her volunteer time, acknowledging that she is already fulfilled. A few weeks later, she called me to tell me that the loving feelings lingered after her dog walks, and her ache for a man started to dissipate. She knew that when she came from this place of empowerment and self-love, she did not need a man anymore. Of course, she still wanted to meet someone, but the feeling of emptiness and lack no longer drove her desire.

As you discover what you can do right now, make a commitment to yourself to do one thing each day to foster those good feelings inside yourself. When you become the solution to your perceived problems, you are more empowered and in control of your destiny.

SELF-HYPNOSIS

Being Happy

Now that you have identified the feelings you want to attain and how you can experience them now, let's reinforce these ideas in your subconscious mind. Before you close your eyes, take the top three things from the previous journaling exercise that you can do right now without a man to get those good feelings and use them in this exercise. Also, be sure to read through the entire exercise before you start.

Close your eyes and take a few deep breaths. Use your favorite deepener to go to the next level of relaxation.

Imagine that you are in an old-time movie theater with plush red-velvet curtains and thick cushioned red seats. You can smell fresh popcorn in the air and feel the sense of excitement that you get in anticipation of a wonderful show. Find a comfortable seat, anywhere you like, and sit back and relax. As you are sitting, you find that you are going deeper into relaxation. On the armrest on your right, you notice a remote control with buttons that read "play," "rewind," "fast-forward," "pause," and "stop." Unlike in the movie theaters that you attended previously, this particular theater allows you to completely control the movie on the screen.

Now think about the first scenario that you put down on your list. As you imagine the thick red-velvet curtains opening, see yourself on the movie screen in that scene. Select "play" and watch the scene while you generate the good feeling. (Pause for a while to do this.)

If you want to increase the good feeling, you will notice that there is a lever on your left armrest with numbers from one to ten. Notice at what level your intensity is and push the lever up higher if you want. When you are finished with the scene and are satisfied with the intensity of your feeling, select the "stop" control and watch the scene go blank.

Now think about the second scenario on your list and go through the same process. Push "play," watch yourself on the screen, and increase the intensity if you like with the lever on the left. (Pause for a while to do this.) Push "stop" when you are finished with that scene.

Now think about the last scenario on your list and repeat the process again. Push "play," watch yourself on the screen, and increase the feeling intensity. (Pause for a while to do this.) Push "stop" when you feel satisfied with that experience.

Now pick your favorite of the three and repeat the process, but this time at the height of the good feeling, imagine yourself moving from the chair and into the movie. Use all of your senses to experience your surroundings: sound, taste, temperature, smell, sights, and more.

You have the power to create joy in your life. You deserve good things. You are meant to be with a loving, psychologically healthy partner. You are important to the world.

Now, as you imagine the feeling and the action, allow yourself to receive. Visualize your true love joining you in the scene while you are already feeling so good. Notice how much more relaxed you are, more authentic, and filled with more self-love and acceptance. You are beginning to realize that you already have the joy that you desire inside, and the man is simply an added element but not the source of your happiness. You are a joyful, happy person. Men are drawn to you because of your wonderful personality and happy disposition. You believe in yourself, and you understand the laws of life. You attract men who treat you with the love and respect you deserve. You are naturally at peace and joyful. You are loving and safe. It is safe to be the real you.

Surround yourself with all of those good feelings and anchor them with your key word, if you'd like, by saying the word three times aloud. You can bring the good feelings back with you even after you've counted up to five and opened your eyes.

Suggestions

Feel free to say these to yourself before you count up to five, if you'd like.

I have an abundance of love inside of me.

My own approval is all that I need.

I attract men who treat me kindly.

I always feel loved.

I deserve a healthy relationship.

I am important to life.

I am perfect just the way I am.

I am whole and complete.

How did you do? Before you continue reading, take out your journal and write down some thoughts about your experience. Other ideas to generate that feeling may flow to your mind, so be sure to make note of them for future reference.

Empowered Desire

Now let us take your desire to the next level. Once you master resolving your unmet inner needs, you must expand your desire to a greater purpose. There is a tenet in the law of attraction, as well as in many religious texts, stating that life's real goal is to serve a purpose for the good of all. In other words, your inner mind is seeking a deeper, more profound spiritual desire.

If you solely focus on yourself and your own life, you might find that you let yourself get lazy, stop doing your hypnosis visualizations, and don't feel compelled to be your best self. Since you are the only one holding yourself accountable, giving up is easy when things get rough. But . . . what if there was something larger than you at stake?

Ultimately, humans have a need to feel connected to the world, to become a part of something larger (even if you are not conscious of this idea yet). Moving beyond your personal and business life, what effect would there be on the world if you stepped into your magnificence?

Accessing Your Inner Greatness

To determine the effect you could have on the world when you get in touch with your inner greatness, let's start small and expand the possibilities. Get into a quiet space and clear your mind.

Take out your journal. On a blank page, write at the top: "Close Friends and Family." Now, think about being your best self and write down how your friends and family would be affected by your doing this. Would they feel more loved and less criticized? Would they be inspired to make changes in their own lives? Write down whatever comes to your mind, even if your thoughts sound far-fetched at the moment.

Now, take that idea to the next level and write at the top of the following blank page: "Coworkers and Acquaintances." Then move on to neighbors and people whom you may not know by name but see frequently on the bus, in the store, or at social events. Put them in the "Community" category. Get creative and come up with some wonderful ideas about how you could influence their lives simply by being a happier, more confident person.

Next, imagine the effect you could have on the world if you expressed all of the love that you have inside yourself. I remember when I used to feel sorry for myself, waiting for Mr. Right to show up. So much wasted time, when I could have focused that energy toward the greater good of the planet. You don't have to wait for permission from a man to be loved or to give love. Think about the people you admire most, and figure out how you can emulate them. You will notice that they didn't sit back and wait for someone to tell them they were okay before they reached out and created change in the world. You are an amazing, powerful person and are capable of more than you can imagine. Expand your idea of what is possible in your life.

Finally, take your effect on the world to an even greater level. On another blank sheet, write "World" at the top. Now imagine that you have affected all of the people you wrote about previously, and the chain reaction that occurred became more powerful and joyful. Write all of the positive things that could come of this.

Here's a story of how this exercise changed one woman's outlook on life: Kimberly, a thirty-eight-year-old administrative assistant, was waiting to have children in order to feel loved. After doing this exercise, she realized that she was holding back on giving love, sitting on the sidelines until a man came to help her start a family. She began to give love to everyone she met, whether in a grocery store or at the gym. Even if she smiled or said a kind word to someone on the elevator, she was doing her part to spread good feelings. Then she took her expression to the next level and sought to fill a greater need in her community. By volunteering at a local battered women's shelter, she felt so much love from the women but also a newfound appreciation for herself. Her inner dialogue shifted as she began to feel fully loved inside, and she met her future husband within months. Now that she is in a relationship, she continues her service to the shelter and does not rely solely on her partner to provide for her emotional needs. Without Kimberly's inner shift, those women would not have benefited from her service. Her relationship with her partner is well balanced, and she doesn't feel desperate to have children. She is no longer anxious about getting engaged, wed, and pregnant but enjoys the here and now with her new love.

You can do the following simple, short visualization anytime you need extra reinforcement or want to be reminded of how influential you can be in the world. You may have picked up this book only to find a way to meet Mr. Right, but you will soon realize that you have much more to gain than merely a healthy romantic relationship. I guarantee that when you finally meet your special guy, you won't

SELF-HYPNOSIS

The Ripple Effect

Be sure to read through the entire exercise before you start.

Close your eyes and imagine that you are in a beautiful place in the center of an imaginary circle surrounded by all of your closest friends and family members. Now think of your good feeling and the color that represents that feeling. Imagine that color flowing out to everyone in the circle. Allow those good feelings to touch and transform them, making them happier and more loved. Then visualize a larger circle outside of them that contains your community and watch that good feeling ripple through them, melting away all of their pain and filling them with good feelings. Next, imagine their good feelings rippling out to everyone in their community, and then everyone in all of those communities transforming lives in their circles of influence. Watch the ripple effect of good feelings move beyond your state and your country to every part of the world. See your beautiful color of good feelings dissolving the suffering in the world.

Now, imagine what the world would be like if everyone felt good about himself or herself. Do you see less hunger and greed and war? Visualize amazing consequences, beyond your wildest dreams. Hold those great feelings and bring them back with you when you count up to five and open your eyes.

feel as if he saved you. In fact, you may be the one to empower him to be his best.

Reinforcing Your Experience

Continue to listen to your daily self-hypnosis program or find some time for your regular visualization. Keep a list of your greatest qualities on a note card and look at it every day. The dashboard in your car or the bathroom mirror is a good place to put love notes to yourself, which will keep your mind focused on your ability to attract the love of your life.

7

A Clear Definition of Love

In real love you want the other person's good.
In romantic love you want the other person.

—Margaret Anderson

The Fairy Tale

Remember when you were a young girl? You may have liked to dress up as a little princess and imagine a prince on a white horse coming to rescue you. Having small crushes on the neighborhood boys, thinking about whom you would marry, and playing house, you were consumed with the idea of being a grown-up. You began your obsession with romantic love.

In your teens, you may have experimented with kissing and putting your name plus the name of your latest crush on the back of your notebook, with TLF (true love forever) next to a big heart. If you were one of the shy girls, as I was, you watched your best girlfriends hold hands with their steadies in the hallways, saw them make out at the lockers, and listened to their myopic conversations about their boyfriend of the week. Perhaps you desperately wanted to be like them and have the experience of love. If you were one of the lucky ones who dated early, you remember the freshness and innocence of that first love. Going steady was simple back then, before sex, ex-husbands and ex-wives, or bigger issues were involved.

As an adult, you may have shifted your idea of romantic love to the fantasy of the perfect wedding day, as you dressed as a bridesmaid too many times and shoved the groom's sister aside to catch the coveted bouquet, which would guarantee your forthcoming nuptials. Your dreams were supported by romantic comedy movies in which the girl gets the guy in the end, and everything works out just fine. All of your problems would be solved if you only had love. Love was the magic remedy to all of life's woes.

Now it is time to wake up from the fantasy. I want you to be open to the word "love" from a different perspective. Our society links love with romance so tightly that we misinterpret its meaning. As a culture, we make the word "love" hard to say without feeling the emotional weight of the sentiment. When the word is said in a romantic situation, it often creates either great expectations or fear in one or both parties.

I hate to break it to you, but romantic love is a fairy tale; real love can only be found inside of you. And although feelings of romantic love seem very real and profound, *it is an illusion that love comes from the other person in the relationship*. In truth, feelings of love are within all of us all the time and, with practice, can be accessed at will.

Wouldn't you feel suddenly free if you let go of the need to get love from someone else? All this time you have been waiting for a man to give you what you already have inside! That is why the search for love can serve as a catalyst for discovering deeper levels of self-awareness. As you search for real love inside yourself, you will begin to distinguish between the surface romantic fantasy and the deep vibration of unconditional love. Instead of attracting superficial relationships, you will gain access to a deeper love without all of the drama.

The Love Delusion

The idea of romantic love was created by man. Since the beginning of time, people mated to propagate the species. Eventually couples were united in arranged marriages based on property. The element of romance was something created by poets, playwrights, and eventually movie producers. The romantic ideas were based on affairs or love doomed because of class differences and early death. This special love was precious, rare, and typically brief. The tales left the "happily ever after" until the end while the main part of the story involved heartache and suffering.

So, why do you seek out something that may cause pain? You are sad when you don't have a relationship and cling to the person you think you love when you have someone in your life, regardless of how he treats you. When love ends, you are in misery again. Why do you do this to yourself? Romantic love is based on *drama*, not on real love. You think you are in love with a person, but really you are addicted to the suffering.

Addicted to Love

Michelle, a single woman in her thirties, came to me obsessed with her last lover and wanting desperately to get over him. She was convinced that she was still in love with her ex, even though he terribly mistreated her. He usually played a push-pull game with her. One day he would push her away, and just when she was ready to move on, he would seduce her back into his life. She felt that breaking off completely with him was almost impossible because she was so in love with him. I asked her to consider the idea that constantly craving another person is not love but an unfulfilled longing for something deeper.

The craving element of romance is a false impression of true love. As you discovered in the previous chapter, your desires go deeper than the surface. The alcoholic is convinced that the good feeling is in the drink, but the high is actually a chemical reaction from the drink mixing with the body's chemistry. Without the body, the intoxication would not be possible. So when you think you love someone romantically, your emotional chemistry mixed with his particular energy creates an illusion of love. The combination of the energies, the actions and reactions from our emotional bodies (our subconscious minds), generates the illusion of a relationship based on the external actions. As long as there is an active charge, the bond holds, no matter how destructive the partnership is to one or both people involved.

The reason that people fall out of love is that something changes inside them and/or their partners. The chemical bond breaks. If the emotional makeup shifts in one or both people, the chemistry will change, and that is when one or the other person loses his or her attraction. There may have been a time in your life when you were doing some personal growth work and the guy you were dating suddenly lost interest. Nothing was said or done differently by you, but something internal shifted. Feeling rejected, you may not have understood at the time that his leaving was a good thing.

I experienced a shift of attraction when I was engaged in my midthirties. This was before I became a hypnotherapist, so my subconscious mind was still filled with lots of false beliefs when I met my fiancé-to-be. Even with my low self-esteem, I managed to attract a man who was crazy about me. I was resistant at first because I really was not used to someone showering me with so much attention, but I conceded, knowing that I needed to break my old pattern of rejecting the nice guys. I convinced myself that I was in love and fantasized that I had finally found Mr. Right.

More in love with the fantasy than the reality of the relationship, we moved in together within three months and got engaged within four. The wedding date was set for six months later. When we first met, we were both into meditation, spirituality, and personal growth. We even went to the same spiritual coach and had sessions together to improve our romantic connection. As the relationship continued, he stopped pursuing his spiritual development and focused on his career. I started to take classes in energy work and concentrated on transforming my inner world. We started to shift in different directions.

The deal breaker for me was that he changed his mind about having children. This was a surface excuse, but I believe the real reason we ended our relationship was because the bond that was initially created wasn't active anymore. The union had been based on neediness, rather than on fullness. I felt rejected. I had to cancel the wedding, return my dress, and sell the condo we'd bought together. The worst part is that we really cared about each other and would miss each other, but those feelings were not enough to sustain a marriage.

During the entire relationship, I'd had a nagging feeling that something was not right. I pushed away the doubts because I really wanted to get married. Hanging on in desperation, I thought he was my last chance. Not a great foundation for lasting relationship, huh? We grew apart energetically, and the original unhealthy bond was gone. My subconscious and his no longer matched; we both changed. Neither of us could be labeled good or bad, just different. Because the internal links had shifted so much, the emotional pain from the breakup was very brief. Intuitively, I knew that the split was a blessing.

Unfortunately, many times only one person shifts, and the other person feels the agony. One addiction remains active, while the other goes numb. People are drawn together by the quality of their subconscious minds. They fit together like puzzle pieces until one or both parties shift their belief systems. This change could happen

over time or very quickly. Regardless of how unhealthy the relationship is, the bond that was formed is usually confused with love.

It Hurts So Good

What most people call love is really agony. The unhealthy parts of
you are drawn to situations that perpetuate the ache from previous
experiences. The familiarity of the hurt, no matter how severe, is
more comforting than the possibility of something new and wonderful. Like any addiction, obsessive love becomes a pattern of behavior
that's hard to break free of.

This discomfort must have an appealing quality to entice people
to keep wanting to experience it. Hidden benefits can infiltrate the
heartache, like getting attention from friends and family or feeling
any emotion at all instead of being numb. I remember the sweet
pain of heartache as being more pleasurable than not having an
object of romantic interest in my life. As long as I felt something,
I was in the game of love and was alive. It was similar to a wild
roller-coaster ride during which I was filled with depths of fear and
heights of joy. I always wanted another ride.

Sadly, many women have endured pain from childhood abuse or
neglect. The dysfunction becomes such a major part of them that
they feel uncomfortable when they're treated nicely. Some gals
act tough with the "I don't need a man" attitude, while inside they
secretly yearn for a loving connection. Many are not even conscious
of the real craving; they simply ignore their deeper feelings because
it hurts too much to feel anything.

The suffering is actually a signal to us that something is out of alignment. Many people seek to remedy the pain with alcohol or food, or
even by mistreating others to lift themselves out of a hole. Whatever
the reason that you may be suffering, find the source of the pain and
address the need so that the feeling can be transformed. Some of the
exercises in this book can help you clear out the unhealthy desires for
love so that you can experience love in its original form.

What Is Love and Where Does It Come From?

You may mistakenly believe that another person holds love to give you, as if he could pour "love energy" into you like warm soup on a cold day. Everyone wants to feel a connection, but your deep mind is convinced that love resides in another person. As you keep searching from lover to lover, you never really get what you want and always yearn for something more. The key is to find a way to access true love within so that you will consistently attract love in the external world. As I discussed in previous chapters, this powerful way of being gives you total control of when you feel love, without waiting for your knight to rescue you from the pain of single-dom.

You may have heard that you must love yourself before someone else can love you, and you wonder how to accomplish that feat. Your mind convinces you that you need proof from the outside world to believe you are worthy. This is a backward way of approaching love because you come from an empty, seeking place, which ultimately can lead to your making bad choices just to fix the perceived problem. In order to discover love within, you first need to understand the foundation of the formula that you created in your early belief system and then re-create a new formula for being loved.

When you were a child, you learned that you got rewarded when you were good and punished when you were bad. You connected the reward with being loved: what you did made you lovable. Most children were never told that they were inherently good, regardless of their behavior, or they probably never would have behaved! You also may have been taught that if you follow certain rules, God will love you. But at the same time, you were told that Jesus loves the sinner. How confusing is this to a young child?

I don't want to get too involved in your spiritual beliefs, but my understanding is that we are already loved by our parents and by God, the universe, and/or the Source of All. God has unconditional love for us. Even when our parents punished us for wrongdoing, they still loved us. The problem was that we were too young to know the difference and interpreted it as a withdrawal of love when they sent us to our rooms.

I thought love had to be demonstrated in order for me to feel accepted. When I was in junior high school, I felt like an outsider. No longer my parent's child, I was a young adult in a very mean world. I saw how girls made alliances. If you were one of lucky ones who got accepted into the cool crowd, you had it made. I was smart, awkward, flat-chested, and dorky, not quite the requirements to be included in the popular-girls group. I sought acceptance from my peers all through my young life. Even more than our families, our peer groups have a strong effect on how we formulate our sense of self.

Later in life, I realized that the cool girls had the same struggles I did. They were also attached to getting attention. In fact, they had a harder time than I did because the whole school knew when they were on the outs with their crowd. The popular girls had a greater need for recognition because they held themselves to much higher standards. As for me, I didn't have to fall far to reach the bottom. I simply blended in with every other name-less, faceless girl in middle school. No matter what your place in the school hierarchy, the need for acceptance and love motivated every individual.

As we grew older, the desire for love transformed into a craving for approval from friends, bosses, coworkers, and neighbors. Of course, we don't want to leave our romantic interests out of the picture because they are the top priority in our desire for approval. Family praise is a never-ending quest, with the same dynamics invariably being repeated. Searching for love from other people will always leave us unsatisfied and wanting more. Finding another source of love, inside ourselves, can empower us in every relationship.

So, *where* can love be found inside? The idea that love is within is probably not new to you. The concept sounds logical enough but often gets lost in translation. Understanding *how* to access love is the key, because love is *everywhere*.

Imagine the power to feel great anytime you need a lift. You can put down the glass of wine or the piece of chocolate cake and stop feeling sorry for yourself because you are alone and single. Instead, you can step into the experience of real love simply by closing your eyes in self-hypnosis.

That's right. The best way to access the love you already have is with visualization (or self-hypnosis). Once you can imagine yourself in a loving partnership, you start to emanate that energy. The spark of love acts as an attraction magnet to draw similar experiences to you. If you hold thoughts of loneliness and impatience, you send that signal out and will receive more experiences that reaffirm that feeling. In order to attract the love of your life, you must practice daily "being-in-love" visualizations to let the universe know you are serious and ready for Mr. Right. The universe will repeatedly bring situations and people to you to match your love vibration.

. The reason this works so effectively is that when you imagine yourself already in love, you come from a place of abundance and wholeness. Remember that old saying "feast or famine"? When you are dating more than one man, doesn't it always seem like everyone is interested in you? When the calls from your lover stop coming, however, other men also seem to lose interest until you get your groove going again. When your mind tells you that there are many opportunities for love, you become a magnet for more attention. Instead of waiting for your calendar to fill up with dates before you allow yourself to feel abundantly loved, why not begin the process yourself?

The feedback I often get from single gals who do the following exercise daily is that men come out of the woodwork. The women get chased down in airports and coffee shops and even approached at business meetings with requests for their phone numbers. They are really feeling the hypno-glow, and everyone can sense their vibrant energy. The good news is that the feeling does not come in a prescription, a fancy dress, or a great skin or hair product. You can create your own love vibe.

Now, before you do this exercise, allow yourself to prepare for meeting the love of your life. Don't try to force an impression or imagine a specific person's face on your dream guy. For best results, simply allow your mind to relax and be open to your inner guidance. Make sure you have your journal ready immediately after the session to record notes on your experience. To make the most of your session, think about a time in your life when you felt truly loved. You can use the memory of a family member or a pet, but try to avoid recalling an old lover. You will use this sensation to greatly affect the depth of love that you have access to in this exercise.

SELF-HYPNOSIS

The Love Magnet

Be sure to read through the entire exercise before you start.

Find a comfortable place to relax, and use your favorite hypnotic-induction technique. Suggestions for inductions: progressive relaxation or taking the stairs from step seven to step one.

Now that you are relaxed, enter a beautiful place. You can be anywhere you like: a beach, a mountain meadow, a forest, a garden. . . . As you imagine yourself standing in this beautiful place, take in all of the sights, smells, and sounds. Really get connected to the natural world around you, the feeling of being one with everything. (Short pause.)

You feel excited anticipation, as if something is going to change in your life. You have a strong desire to discover love within yourself and to attract the love of your life. In order to do this, you know that you must locate where true love exists in the deepest realms of your mind. Take a deep breath and imagine a place in this peaceful setting to visualize yourself sitting down for a moment. Let your mind take you back to a time when you felt truly loved. Think of that time and bring forward those feelings of unsurpassed love.

Imagine a beautiful golden light energy growing inside your heart as your feelings become stronger. Allow the light to become a large lotus flower that opens up and expands around your entire upper body. Keep thinking of that memory and expand that love around you until you are fully enveloped in a warm, golden light of love. Be sure to keep focusing on the source of this light, which rests in your heart and in that beautiful lotus flower. Imagine that light grounding you, expanding all around your body, and sinking deeply into the floor beneath you. You can imagine the ends of the light turning into the shape of roots that connect you to the earth, drawing the wonderful power of the earth upward to keep you solid and strong.

When you are at the height of this feeling, simply say these words to yourself or aloud: "I feel love fully and completely right now and call out to my beloved, who matches this pure, love energy, to come into my life."

Picture in your mind millions of sparks of this golden light moving outward into the world, sending out the signal for your true love to find you. As you patiently wait, you see a bigger light begin to move toward you from the distance.

As the bright light comes closer to you, you see that it transforms into the shape of a person moving toward you. The person in the light holds that same love energy that you do.

Stand up as he comes closer and walk toward this wonderful being of light. You may or may not be able to make out exactly what he looks like, and that is okay. Allow your mind to show you what you are ready to see.

When you are only a few feet apart, imagine him taking one of your hands in his. Feel his kindness, his warmth, and his love matching the energy that you have been creating all along. Imagine the golden energy in your heart space begin to expand out to his heart. You notice that he has the same golden essence around him, and both of your energies make a perfect match. Feel the exchange of energy, knowing that you are not receiving any more love than you already have, you are simply feeling his love in addition to yours, as if you are a cup that is filled to overflowing.

Now watch the energy start to swirl around both of you, creating a magnetic attraction so that your subconscious mind is clear on what you want and how you want to feel with your partner.

Breathe in and out and really get a sense of his unique energy mixed with all of your good feelings. (If you're recording this session, pause to give yourself time to enjoy the connection.)

You can ask him any questions you like, such as his name, what is preventing him from entering your life right now, where the two of you will meet, or any other clear directives from your inner guidance. (If you're recording this session, pause to give yourself time to ask your questions.)

Now say good-bye to your love partner, knowing that your time together on earth will begin very soon. Allow the magnetic attraction to stay in place, and feel your heart become lighter and lighter and lighter. You are ready to let love in . . .

Remember that you can bring all of these feelings back with you even after you open your eyes. Count up to five and become wide awake; you feel good and you remember everything that you witnessed.

Suggestions

Feel free to say these to yourself before you count up to five, if you'd like.

I am open and ready for love.

I believe in myself.

I have wonderful, attractive qualities.

Men find me attractive.

I have a great personality and a good heart.

I love men, and they love me.

I am learning to listen to my intuition.

My intuition is growing stronger each and every day.

I am familiar with the internal nudges that direct me to where I need to be to meet my true love.

My true love is waiting for me.

Journaling

Free-Form Writing

This can be done each time you do the Love Magnet exercise. Write down all of the thoughts that come to your mind after you open your eyes. Don't judge or edit your comments; simply allow your mind-chatter to empty out onto the paper. If you reread what you've written after a few days, you will notice that your impressions become clearer and that doubts are less prevalent in your thinking. Most people meet their partners within thirty days of doing continuous daily visualizations.

Success Stories

Rachel, a life coach in her late twenties, had been playing the online dating game for years. She picked up my *Attract the Love of Your Life* visualization program at a wellness fair I attended, and she faithfully listened to it every day. Within three weeks, she found herself on a date with someone who was not superficially her type, but she gave him a chance because she had a certain feeling about him. A few minutes into their coffee date, she realized that his face matched the image in her visualization. Although she normally would not have given him a second date, she followed her inner guidance and went out with him again. After about a month, they were smitten, and the last that I heard, she was engaged to him.

Karlie, a thirty-six-year-old financial consultant, felt invisible to men until she started doing daily visualizations. She began to feel the love inside her and reported having so many men ask her out that she was confused about which one was best for her. It was nice to have choices, but she felt a little overwhelmed. I told her to make sure she wrote down a list of what she wanted in a man. After compiling her list, she easily let go of the mismatches and discovered the guy who fit best with her. A year later, she was happily in a long-term relationship and planning their wedding.

Barbara, a fifty-two-year-old bakery owner, attended one of my workshops at a singles' event in Denver. I conducted the Love Magnet exercise with a group of over a hundred single men and women. Barbara wrote to me a few weeks later to thank me for the visualization and told me that she met her true love one hour later at the event. He was wearing the same shirt she imagined and he said the same words she heard during the session. She was amazed at how powerful this process was, especially after having been single for so long. I have heard similar stories of immediate results from many of my customers and clients.

Some Cautions

Even though some people meet their true love swiftly after doing the Love Magnet exercise, use caution. Be careful not to fall for the first guy you meet after doing only a few visualizations. He *may* be the right one for you, but don't get ahead of yourself. Many clients get fooled easily when they are still so focused on fixing their perceived problem of being single. My best advice is to take your time. Your inner guidance may show you a face that becomes familiar to you in the real world, but you could be drawn to a guy you need to date to prepare you for the right one. I highly recommend doing the Love Magnet exercise for thirty consecutive days before you jump into any serious relationship.

Don't worry if you don't meet Mr. Right within thirty days of doing this visualization. I put this exercise in the middle of the book to make sure that you've had some practice, but you still may have some clearing to do before he arrives. The purpose is not to find him immediately but to train your subconscious mind to realize that love is already inside you. Keep training and keep believing in yourself. The second section of this book will reveal some additional road-blocks that may still remain deep in your mind.

Reinforcing Your Experience

Practice daily self-hypnosis and always include a visualization of meeting your perfect mate. Insert suggestions to retrain your mind from those old, false beliefs to new, empowered ideas. Review your "man order" every day.

PART TWO

Taking Action: Roadblocks on Love's Highway

Thought is the blossom; language the bud;
action the fruit behind it.

—Ralph Waldo Emerson

Once you clear away the false core beliefs about love in your subconscious, you can increase your love magnetism through your actions. Your physical and emotional acts either support your intentions or work against them. What you do and feel is the unspoken language that interacts with the creative force. To act, you must be willing to move outside of your comfort zone. You cannot find true love by waiting at home. Even Cinderella had to get herself to the ball to find her handsome prince. By taking the right actions, you tell the creative force that you are serious about finding love.

In addition to taking physical action, you need to address the emotional reactions in your body so that you can clear away past pain to allow love into your life. Emotional struggles can cause you to hold back on expressing yourself fully, which inhibits your ability to attract your true partner. Self-hypnosis can help you change your physical and emotional habits to be consistent with your highest desires.

8

Don't Give Your Feelings the Cold Shoulder

All emotions are pure which gather you and lift you up; that emotion is impure which seizes only one side of your being and so distorts you.

—Rainer Maria Rilke

Thinking Positive When You're Not Feeling Positive

How many books have you read on positive thinking? You may have heard your married friends repeatedly say, "Just think positive!" in their cheery, smug, *I-already-have-a-man* voice. The problem is that it is impossible to remain consistently upbeat. If you have been exposed to a lot of positive-thought literature, you may tend to judge yourself harshly when you are feeling bad. This leads to more feelings of negativity. But emotions are not inherently good or bad—they are what they are. Your feelings have a powerful influence in helping you work with the creative energy to attract your life circumstances, and they should be managed with care.

Some advice I have heard on the self-help circuit is to quickly change your negative thoughts into positive thoughts, and if you are feeling bad, to start to feel good. The basis for this theory is logical. If you think and feel negatively all the time, you will attract more things to feel terrible about. Another layer to this equation often gets overlooked, though, and, if ignored, keeps people in a state of suffering, regardless of their attempts to be positive.

The problem with the advice to stay positive is that most people only pretend to be upbeat on the surface, while their deep inner minds are still in turmoil. They shut themselves off from the negative emotions because they know these are "bad," and they don't want to attract anything "bad" into their lives. So they ignore the impulses and shove them under a rug.

Imagine a crying child coming into a room in search of comfort. Would you tell the child to go away and shut up? Well, that's what you tend to do to your feelings. If you reject your darker feelings, you may attempt to drown them with television, music, food, drugs, alcohol, or sex. This is because the subconscious mind learns to seek a temporary fix, regardless of whether the activity is good for you. You may have learned to cover up your emotions and pretend that everything is okay, although deep inside you feel terrible. Those feelings never really dissolve, and they begin to fester and grow inside of you.

The Dangers of Ignoring or Rejecting Your Feelings

There are many dangers to ignoring your feelings. For one, the unease can turn to disease in your body. The stress of suppressing anger, resentment, or fear creates cells in your body called free radicals. Your body's natural immune system battles these dangerous cells but cannot fend off constant attacks. Some scientists link this process to cancer, ulcers, heart disease, and other medical conditions. You may have witnessed this happening with a people-pleasing person who ended up developing a terminal illness or the uncle who never had much to say and who suffered from a massive heart attack.

Suppressing your feelings also leads to creating a fake persona, and the guys whom you go out with never know who you really are. This often happens because a woman doesn't want to make waves when she first starts to date someone. She doesn't stand up for herself and simply hopes that the man will change. Eventually, if the relationship does last, the woman is stuck in a pattern that makes her feel resentful and bitter toward her partner. Fearing the loss of the man, she will suck it up and put up with mistreatment. She then blames her partner for not honoring her, when she originally did not respect herself enough to maintain her boundaries.

Because feelings are of the body, the flow of energy inside you must be in alignment with the clarity of your mental vision. If you think you want a relationship but feel sad about being single, you are sending mixed signals to the universe about what you want to create—*feeling sad and single*. Your feelings are your true message to the formless energy, asking it to bring back more of the same to you. What vibration of energy do you send out and receive in your life? If you want to attract love, you must find a way to authentically feel the emotion of love, regardless of your current circumstances.

Now, you don't want to simply reject those unhappy feelings as being bad or wrong; you must learn to understand and heal them so that they no longer fester underneath the surface. The lighter you feel, the more easily you can realize your true desires. You cannot speed up the process by skipping over your feelings in order to get a man. You will end up with temporary results and will unconsciously return to old behaviors because of the unmet needs of your internal pain.

Nancy was a forty-year-old accountant who had been divorced twice. She had been trained to hide her emotions from an early age, when it was dangerous for her to express herself. Her father was an alcoholic and would beat her if she whined or tried to defend her position. After a while, she accepted whatever he said and took on the persona of a nice girl who obeyed him. Each of her marriages lasted for only a year before her husbands had affairs. She found out later that they both had felt that she was too accommodating, and they got bored.

On the other hand, Christine was highly disagreeable with her men. Even when she agreed with them, this thirty-two-year-old sales associate pretended not to acquiesce because she didn't want to be perceived as weak. She initially came to me because she didn't know why she always caused friction in her relationships. She truly wanted to connect with the men in her life, but something inside her automatically rejected those feelings. When she was a little girl, her mother never gave her any approval. Even when Christine got good grades, her mother found something wrong. Christine's sensitivity to her mother's verbal abuse hardened over time and eventually led to her repeating her mom's behavior. Unbeknownst to Christine, she was simply afraid to let love in, and she pushed away men before they could reject her.

Being too pleasing or too disagreeable are ways that we ignore our true feelings. Even though the sensations of sadness, rejection, anger, and fear are suppressed, they still lurk beneath the surface. To change your emotions when they come up doesn't resolve anything but simply creates a cycle of misery. You forget your true essence and become a stranger to your own self.

Another trap that singles fall into is forgetting how wonderful they are and pretending to have a different personality to win the affection of their love interest. After surviving the battle of puberty, I emerged into my twenties with a new identity. Because I received better social feedback in high school when I didn't have the best grades in class and acted hip with my lettered drill-team jacket, I decided that being dumb and cool worked with men. I pretended that I didn't want a relationship. I had plenty of men in my little black book, whom I had fooled into thinking that I wasn't brainy and boring. That worked for a while, until I started to date a guy named Bill who had known me in high school, and he blew my cover.

He knew that I was really smart, and he liked the person I had been in high school—sweet, quiet, the girl-next-door type. Unfortunately, I had made up my mind that being a cool, popular airhead was more appealing to men. Afraid to let my vulnerability show, I had become far removed from my true self. I was convinced that I had to hide the dorky part of me in order to be accepted by a man. Bill could not stand who I was pretending to be, and I ultimately drove him away. We had a special connection, and I always regretted how I acted back in those days. He was one of the few men who'd loved me for who I really was. He simply rejected the false persona that I showed him. He was one of my greatest teachers. To this day, he does not know the effect he had on me.

I remember a friend giving me some feedback about the situation, which has stuck with me to this day. She said, "Who you really are and how you act are so different. You pretend to be a fun girl who wants to play the field, but then you tell us privately that you really want to meet someone special, get married, and have children. The jerks are attracted to the fun girl, and the nice guys believe you are not interested in a relationship." This advice was hard to hear, but it clarified everything to me about what was happening in my love life. At this point, I began the long process of rediscovering my true self.

Discovering Your True Feelings

Not being able to identify your true feelings is one of the biggest roadblocks to a happy relationship. You will consistently attract the wrong man if you base your decisions on your false, superficial self. In this book, I have often said that your feelings are the magnets that attract or repel love in your life. Addressing your emotions is probably the most important element stressed in this book.

Feelings are powerful because they are wordless. Verbal communication is so limited. Have you ever tried to describe what ice cream tastes like? You can describe textures, flavors, colors, and even the sweetness, but your words can never match the actual experience of eating the ice cream. The emotions play a powerful role because they send strong messages to attract more of what you are feeling, in a way that transcends your vocabulary.

You immediately get a sense of a room as you enter without anyone saying a word to you. You can get impressions of people by the looks on their faces and the energy in the room. Your internal radar works with your felt sense. Isn't it interesting that when a guy smiles and says he is going to call you to get together again, you can sense when he is lying? You can pick up on whether his intentions match his words. How about politicians? You can sense the people who seem to be more truthful than others because of your gut feelings.

People always communicate with one another through their feeling minds. You have the power to lift up a room or drag the whole place down with your emotions. What you feel is more important than what you say. Have you ever comforted a friend without words? Just sitting quietly near him or her can be very nurturing. Even your pets know when you are feeling down, and they come to your side with those sad eyes, wishing they could help. If they are small enough, they can curl up on your lap and transform your mood. Unspoken gestures between you and others influence your life experiences.

You may fool people for a little while with a fake smile, but eventually your true feelings will be transparent. Most of the time, people already see through the facade but don't have the courage to tell you. You cannot hide from your emotions; they will always reach the surface and rear their heads.

How to Embrace Your Feelings with Power

When I talk about emotions, I avoid describing them as good or bad. They are simply how we feel. Many communication courses teach

us to share our feelings by saying, "When you do that, I feel _____."
The reason this is so powerful is that no one can or should tell us to
feel anything other than what we are authentically feeling.

There is nothing to be ashamed of when you are sad, depressed,
or angry. Without those uncomfortable feelings, you would not enjoy
the pleasant ones, like joy, peace, or bliss. Unfortunately, societal
judgments make expressing your actual sentiments quite difficult.
Labeling your feelings good or bad creates resistance to completely
accepting yourself for who you are and how you feel. Thus, we shun
the "bad" and pretend that everything is all right.

Instead of suppressing the unpleasant feelings, you can embrace
them with power and learn how to work with them to transform them
into something that is more comfortable. The reason the emotions are there in the first place is to alert you that something is
out of order. Learning to recognize whether your feelings are truly
intuitive nudges or old worn-out fears is the trickiest part of this
process.

When you feel an emotion, your mind immediately starts to
develop a story line about what that feeling means. Flashbacks from
past experiences or familiar worries will appear in your thinking.
The impressions, based on the past, become fully viable again in
the present and can overcome you. Many people who suffer from
depression are stuck in a loop of fear, tension, and pain that they
relive over and over again. As if you are on autopilot, these feelings become a habit long after you have forgotten their true origin.
The sensations become so familiar that the uncomfortable becomes
comfortable, and you may resist any attempt to transform them into
something different. Even if the result of changing them logically
seems pleasant, the emotions are so entrenched in your ego that
you feel as if you may lose a valuable part of yourself if you let them
go. Ridiculous, you may think, but this is how all emotional patterns
have remained in your life for decades.

To fully face your feelings—the ugliness, the pain, and the
sorrow—is the only way for you to be a powerful creator of your

life. Your feelings are the root of your suffering and the source of your joy. Instead of riding them like the rapids flowing down a steep river, you can become one with the water and make it still so that your mind and body can drift along a quiet, rolling stream.

In preparation for the next exercise, have your journal ready and find a quiet place so that you won't be disturbed. Please allow at least forty-five minutes to go through the entire process. I don't want you to start the exercise and have to run off in the middle without completing it. Read through all of the steps before you begin, to be clear about each step so that you get the best results.

Journaling

The Seven-Step Feeling Exercise

1. *Feel*. Think about an uncomfortable feeling that you are familiar with in your everyday life. For example, you may have an emotion such as loneliness, frustration, or sadness concerning your single status, a bad breakup, your last bad date, or a recent rejection. You may feel all of these emotions and more, but pick one for this exercise. Concentrate on that feeling. (Don't worry, I am not going to keep you there.)

2. *Find*. Now find the feeling inside your body. Close your eyes and scan your body. Where do you feel the uncomfortable sensations physically?

3. *Describe*. Describe the feeling to yourself. Is it tight? Moving? Hard? Soft? Rigid? Sharp? Make that feeling a dark color. Create a shape or an image that represents that feeling. Some of my clients have made the feeling look like body armor, a sharp knife, a hard rock, and a jelly orb; visualize whatever you like.

4. *Write the story*. Now that you have a handle on what this feeling is, open your eyes for a moment and write a description of what this feeling means to you. There is no right or wrong way to do this; simply take note of whatever flows through your mind (example: I feel this way every time a guy doesn't call. This ache is the pain of loneliness; I am so alone). Continue writing until your mind starts to slow down or until you have written one or two pages. Understand the story line that keeps this feeling activated.

5. *Ask*. Close your eyes again and imagine that you can talk to this feeling. Tell it that you are now aware of the thoughts that created it. You can ask how old you were when you first started to feel this way. Ask the object/sensation what would make it feel better. Listen to your first response. The answer will come in a word or a phrase (examples: safety, love, confidence, and so on).

6. *Receive*. Now bring a new, lighter feeling into your experience based on your answer in step 5. Think of a time in your life when you felt loved, safe, or confident (or another feeling) and make that energy a light color like blue, yellow, white or pink. As you remember that time, bring up the good feelings and imagine that dark shape you created (in step 3) in your body being filled with these new feelings of love, safety, confidence, and so on. Watch the old, dark shape transform into something pleasant or completely dissolve into the good feeling color. Fill yourself up with the new feeling and anchor your key word if you like, or anchor a new word to use as a trigger in the future by saying the word three times now.

> *Option*: If you have trouble transforming the old feeling, imagine your adult self giving your younger self a big hug (at whatever age you were when you determined this feeling to have first occurred).

7. *Release*. Scan your body to determine whether there are any remnants of the old feeling left. Imagine the remains being like thick pockets of smoke that float upward out of your body. (You can ask your higher self, angels, God, or a greater power to assist in the removal.)

To finish the release, open your eyes and write the following in your journal:

When I was [previous circumstance that caused the old feeling], I used to feel like a [shape, sensation].

I discovered that I really wanted [new feeling], and now I have access to this [new feeling] anytime I want. I no longer need [the old circumstance] to feel [desired feeling].

Example: When I was *rejected*, I used to feel like *I had a gaping hole in my stomach being pierced with knives*. I discovered that I really wanted *acceptance*, and now I have access to this *feeling of loving acceptance* anytime I want. I no longer need *a man's approval* to *feel loved and accepted*.

Be sure to include these supportive phrases as suggestions in future hypnosis exercises. If you are uncertain as to whether you did the exercise as directed, read the success story below as an example to follow.

Matt, a thirty-nine-year-old engineer, was familiar with anxiety. He was the child of alcoholic parents and spent his whole life feeling that he was always walking on eggshells and suffering as a result of it. As a child, he was not allowed to cry or express emotions or he would face corporal punishment or bed without dinner. He learned to suppress his anger and not to fight back, and he lived in constant fear. When he started dating, he had the same anxiety. Despite his low self-esteem and extreme anxiety, this handsome man was always approached by women, and his coworkers offered to fix him up on blind dates. He really wanted to explore dating but experienced panic whenever he was around someone new. The women he dated usually took advantage of his good nature. He never stood up for himself, in fear of being cut off from the little affection these women showed him. On the verge of reaching forty and desperately wanting to change his life, he contacted me.

In one session, we worked with his anxiety. Matt saw the tension in his body as a block of lead sitting on his chest that reduced his ability to breathe and created a tingling sensation down his arms, making them feel weak. When he asked the feeling what it needed, he said the word "safety." I had him identify a time in his life when he felt secure, and he could not think of anything. After a few minutes, I asked him whether he had a pet. His face lit up and he smiled as he described his yellow Lab named Lacey. I had him think of Lacey and imagine a yellow color dissolving away the block of lead on his chest, relieving the tension in his arms and allowing him to breathe. He realized that he had begun to feel this way when he was six years old. I also had him imagine his adult self giving his six-year-old child self a warm embrace. He mentioned that this was extremely powerful for him because his parents never gave him hugs.

Immediately after the session, he felt a sense of relief from the tense feelings. He visualized going to a crowded restaurant on a date, and he reported that he did not have the same old tension he'd felt before we did the process. At our next session, Matt reported that the old feeling had never come back, and he'd even asked a girl at work out for lunch. He said that this was the first time he had ever approached a woman without feeling anxious, and he thought I was a miracle worker. I told him that he was actually the one who had done all of the work with his own incredible mind power.

Everyone has stuck feelings from the past that create discomfort in his or her life. If you react one way to a certain event, your subconscious mind will repeat the same reaction again in any remotely similar situation. *Even after you have grown up, the feelings remain at the age you were when they were initially created in your deep mind's memory.*

So if a young girl was embarrassed in front of her second-grade class while presenting her book report, the shame feeling is locked into her at seven years old. As an adult surrounded by colleagues in a board meeting, when she is asked to give a report on her department's progress, this adult woman may shrink down emotionally to her seven-year-old self and respond in a similar fashion to how she did in second grade.

The Seven-Step Feeling exercise gives you insight and power over these old stored responses so that you can transform them. Instead of reacting as usual, you interrupt the patterns and discover a way to face, embrace, and heal the feelings or the stored traumas in a few minutes. At the time the feeling was stored, you may not have had access to the comfort, love, or safety you needed, so this energy was left with an unmet yearning. When you do this exercise, you are completing the gap of what you needed to feel better. So instead of waiting for a guy to come along to complete you, you've done it yourself. As you shed layers of these past emotions through this exercise and other processes in this book, you will begin to feel lighter and more powerful in every aspect of your life.

How Empowered Feelings Can Improve Your Relationships

Now that you have a handle on working effectively with your emotions, think about how becoming free from past emotional baggage can affect your love life. How will your experience be different now that you've gotten rid of that old feeling? Take out your journal and have some fun describing how your world will be transformed without the extra weight of heavy emotions. Specifically, describe what future relationships will be like when you are in complete control of what you feel and why.

For most people, freeing themselves from old toxic emotions allows them to step out of their comfort zones a bit more. They find themselves going out to more social events and even approaching potential mates for the first time. By regaining control of your life, you stop retreating from or tiptoeing around people and begin to fully express your opinions. When you used to say yes out of fear, now you stand your ground and let go of the need to please to keep the peace.

Initially, you may have been trained to disguise your feelings to avoid provoking conflict, but many of the healthiest relationships are created because of the raw honesty that partners share with each other. By facing situations in the present, people experience fewer chances of resentment building and fewer episodes of sudden aggression. Your family, friends, and potential partners get to know the real you. You build confidence by honoring and respecting yourself and your own feelings. As you become more intimate with your emotions, you increase your ability to be truly connected with a partner. You will discover even more about yourself as you learn to distinguish between old patterns and intuitive nudges.

True Intuitive Nudges vs. Old Pain Resurfacing

Every uncomfortable feeling in your body does not always have to be transformed. Your deep mind has a wealth of knowledge, even though you seem to use it only for repetitive tasks and habitual emotional responses. Each person has an intuitive ability, which is more developed in some people than in others. This intuition is a combination of all of the knowledge accumulated in the deep mind throughout an individual's life, as well as his or her spiritual energy. As I mentioned earlier, people are reading one another's subconscious minds all the time, so you are picking up impressions from a collective mind as well as from your own. You may receive these "hits" through any of your five senses, but primarily, people sense things kinesthetically (with their feelings).

Have you ever gone out on a date with someone, and even though he seemed "good on paper," there was something odd about this person that you couldn't quite identify? Or have you ever sensed that a guy was cheating on you, without having any concrete evidence? Your deep mind is at work, giving you a nudge to help you out. Obviously, these feelings don't need to be transformed because they can be useful. If you are one of the fortunate people who often has access to this amazing sense, I suggest that you keep a diary of the feelings (describe the sensations) and the results. Anytime you sense that something is a little "off," you can work with the feeling to find answers.

Use your feelings as a gypsy uses a crystal ball. Talk to the feeling and ask for insight: "What are you trying to tell me?" You can either have a dialogue in your mind or free-write the dialogue in your journal. Allow your wiser inner self to speak to you and give you direction. You don't need to spend hundreds of dollars on a psychic when you have a mystic inside of you.

To determine whether you are sensing old baggage or intuition takes practice. Many times, uncomfortable feelings are simply growing pains. When you move out of your comfort zone, your mind automatically reacts with fear. Some people go through changes more gracefully than others do. The key is that instinctive feelings are more pure and unfamiliar, unlike the old baggage that you notice all the time. Unfortunately, there is no rule book for measuring feelings, and you must learn to discern what they mean for yourself.

Many times when you break old dating habits, you feel a bit uncomfortable if a man showers you with love and adoration. How do you know whether you are just timid about being loved or are picking up a vibe that something isn't quite right with this fellow? Only you can answer this question. You can do the Seven-Step Feeling exercise anytime you need clarity.

DeAnne, a thirty-eight-year-old legal assistant, came to me after ending a very bad marriage with a man who verbally abused her. She was rebuilding her self-esteem and had started to attract men who treated her nicely. She noticed that as we worked together and her confidence grew, her feelings of fear around men who came on too strong had greatly decreased. She was afraid of being loved because she didn't think she deserved a good relationship. Her anxiety grew when a man approached her with too much love. In this case, we worked with the anxious sensations and transformed them so that she was open enough to let love in. The uncomfortable feeling wasn't her intuition telling her that the guy was bad, but was simply her old conditioned behavior of allowing only abusive men in her life.

Pamela had a different experience. A forty-two-year-old English teacher, she had been amicably divorced and was ready to date again. She felt confident about herself but didn't believe she could find love again at her age. Having a balanced life with work and social activities, she was not in a rush to meet her man but definitely preferred being in a relationship. She started to date a guy named Tom, who quickly fell for her. During their courtship, he sent flowers every Monday to the school where she worked. At first, she was flattered by all of his attention, but something held her back from falling for him too fast. She told me that she couldn't consciously verify her awkward feelings, but she knew something was off.

He pressured the physical aspect of the relationship, but Pamela did not concede. She was holding off until she knew that she felt the same way about him. Then, about six weeks into their courtship, she discovered why she'd felt so resistant. She found out that he had some financial problems and had separated from his wife of fifteen years a few months earlier. He had lied about his name and was not who he portrayed himself to be. Her intuition was telling her that he was too good to be true, and her instinct was right.

So, which story line will you follow? How do you really know whether your feelings are intuition or not? Sometimes you just don't know. What I can say is that every person's experience is unique. The more you get to know yourself, your patterns, your feelings, and your beliefs, the more easily you can discriminate between healthy and neurotic situations and make the right decisions. If you experience fear when you meet a nice man, talk to your feelings and ask them for insight. Trust yourself. You are wiser than you know.

Harnessing Your Feelings to Attract Your Heart's Desire

By the time you reach this point in the book, you may already have released a plethora of old story lines and feelings. You might have found this section to be quite easy. Have you noticed that people now ask you what you are doing and say that you seem *different*? You may have seen changes right away or only now after doing the Seven-Step Feeling exercise. Either way, do not fret. There are plenty of steps ahead to help you let more love in.

Many of my clients report to me that they feel weird (in a good way). On the surface, they don't sense much change until they run into a circumstance that formerly made them uneasy. They experience a disconnection from their old suffering and realize, "Wow, it's working!"

I remember the first time I did hypnotherapy. I had struggled with dating for such a long time that I was open to anything to bring me out of my funk. I asked a hypnotherapist to help me let go of my need for approval from men. I felt good after the session but really didn't notice any dramatic changes. Later that week, I was expecting a call from a new guy whom I had been dating. He'd told me on our last date that he would be in touch with me to schedule a time to get together that weekend. With no phone call by late Thursday afternoon, I knew I had been blown off. My typical response would have been to feel awful, sick to my stomach, and to spiral down into negative mind-chatter about how I would be alone forever—not a fun experience. This time, however, when I realized that the guy wasn't going to follow through on his word, I simply shrugged my shoulders and let the whole thing go. I even tried to drum up those old feel-sorry-for-myself emotions but couldn't find them. I felt as if someone had taken out my pain as if it were a tumor—it was gone.

When you do these exercises, you may notice profound changes immediately or subtle changes over time. Each individual is different. Michael, a forty-five-year-old real estate agent, came to me needing help with his anxiety. He said that after the hypnosis session, the uncomfortable feeling was still slightly there, but it dissolved completely over the next twenty-four hours.

Similar to clearing your mind of unwanted beliefs, you also need to keep your feelings clear and focused, free from distraction. If you think positive but feel lousy, you won't be sending an unmixed signal to the universe to attract Mr. Right. Your deep mind will be more open and receptive to new, positive changes in your love life when you become lighter emotionally.

You have learned that you can embrace your feelings with power and use them to help you experience the real you. Now you can push away the sweets, the cigarettes, and the glass of wine and really start to feel again. All of your feelings have value, just as every part of you can be a teacher for your growth.

Without your feelings, you couldn't be in love, enjoy a sunset, laugh with friends, and cry at sad movies. An integral part of your life that makes living rich, powerful, and wonderful, feelings can be your greatest gift. Many depressed people cannot feel at all. Conditioned to numb themselves to life's perceived pains, they let the world swallow them up. By acknowledging your true emotions, you become a powerful creator of your destiny. Someone once told me that the more deeply you feel your pain, the greater the heights of joy you can experience. If you can learn to manage and transform the pain, think about how much happiness lies ahead.

There is a difference between thinking positive and being positive. I see many people use affirmations but not engage the feeling behind the words that they say. Their efforts are like going to church and repeating the same prayers because you know them so well but feeling disconnected from their meaning. Thoughts and words have a certain vibration and can help you attract the things you desire. But if you don't match your will with your feelings, you won't experience the full power of your mind.

Saying that you believe your true love is on his way while at the same time feeling discouraged lessens the effect. On the other hand, you cannot pretend to feel good when you are down. The only way to transform your life experience is to find ways to foster the emotions you desire within yourself. As described earlier, *feel*, *act*, and then you will *receive* your desire. Accept all of your emotions as great teachers, and, as you work with them, you will become more empowered.

Reinforcing Your Experience

Continue to do your daily self-hypnosis with suggestions. Be sure to incorporate any new suggestions that you uncovered in this section. If your list of affirmations gets too long, you can review and edit as you move through the process. Practice matching the words that you speak with feelings. By being present and conscious of your words, you learn to be more vigilant in aligning them with your intention of attracting love.

9

Seduction, Substitutions, and Settling

There is no passion to be found playing small—in settling for a life that is less than the one you are capable of living.

—Nelson Mandela

Actions Speak Louder Than Words

You may have heard the advice to pay attention to how your man acts, instead of to what he says, to understand his true intentions. His claims of love for you don't matter when he's not available for Saturday night dates, he doesn't call, or you find him cheating. You learn that his words are cheap. Just as if you say that you love yourself but continue to take actions that don't match self-love, you are not walking your talk. Giving away your body freely, dating men who mistreat you, or abusing your body with alcohol and food are not acts of honoring yourself. Your actions reveal your true inner feelings.

Your behavior affects the quality of the relationships that you attract. The most common foible is to continue to date unavailable men to fill up your social calendar or to fulfill your sexual needs until "the one" comes along. Having a temporary man is like settling for a bottle of Colt 45 in a paper bag when you really want Dom Pérignon in a fine champagne flute. Unfortunately, this tendency sends a strong signal to the subconscious that a second-rate mate is all you deserve. Your *actions* must be congruent with the desire for a healthy relationship in order to attract "the one" into your life.

On the other hand, you may not have dated in years. If you haven't made any attempt to meet new people, your inaction is blocking love. You cannot meet your man if you are always sitting at home alone. Unless your true love turns out to be the delivery guy, you have to get out there! When you take action toward what you really want, love will meet you in the middle.

Every action you take, whether minor or significant, sends an unspoken signal to your subconscious mind and to the universe. There are no unrecorded actions. Everything has a cause and an effect. Your actions can reinforce or dilute beliefs of self-acceptance in your deep mind. If you are having an affair with a married man, you reinforce opinions in your deep mind that you are not worthy of real love. Any self-hypnosis exercises you perform to reverse those thoughts are mitigated by your opposing actions. If you think you are being clever by secretly having an affair with a married man, think again. Your subconscious mind is always watching and responding to your thoughts *and* actions.

You may try to convince yourself that dating a man who won't commit is okay for now because you simply want the company. If you continue the behavior, though, you are sending mixed signals to your deep mind and ultimately will attract more men who won't commit. The actions you take are so powerful, they override any self-hypnosis exercises that steer your mind in the direction of real love. Many times, my clients have told me that their dream guys showed up as soon as they dumped their sex buddies.

The Dangers of Mr. Right Now

Having fun with Mr. Right Now, instead of the one you were meant to love, is a dangerous game. Not only can your romantic dealings be physically damaging if you are with someone abusive, but your actions can be emotionally devastating as well. Everyone gets lonely and needs attention and affection and to be taken out to a nice dinner. There is nothing wrong with casually dating and meeting new people. The danger is when you become *addicted* to the Mr. Right Nows and continue to spend time with men who don't meet your criteria for "the one."

You may argue that you don't want to be rigid about what you're looking for, and maybe Mr. Right Now can turn into Mr. Right. Yes, that is a possibility, but are you simply justifying your behavior? Your subconscious blocks to love show up in mysterious ways. You may be thinking and feeling more upbeat and confident, but if you accept less than what you want, you are sabotaging your efforts to attract love.

You receive a hidden benefit when you date Mr. Right Nows, and your deep mind will continue to rationalize your actions. Some perks are obvious. You get to go out and feel attractive. Another more subtle benefit you receive is avoiding meeting new people. By occupying your time with the wrong guys, you could be cushioning yourself from real intimacy.

Seduction by the Temporary Man

So maybe you think that you aren't hiding out, using the temporary man as a barrier to real love. You just want a little action until your prince arrives. These "temps" who fill your social calendar and your bed come in many forms—the friend with benefits, the one-night stand,

and that jerky ex-boyfriend who keeps coming back for more. The only reason you would continue this behavior is to block love from entering your life, consciously or unconsciously.

Temporary men are a vehicle to distract you from true closeness. Who wouldn't love the connection of a great friend who is sexually compatible and can be your date of choice at any social event that arises? These sex buddies are very convenient to have on your shelf, ready to pluck. They are familiar, they may be kind to you, and they fit in your life like a comfortable old shoe. A man like this may get too cozy (and may even move in), but he is definitely *not* your dream guy. The danger, of course, is that you postpone the romance you desire and become complacent with the status quo.

Maybe you cannot resist the pull of the sex buddy's attraction, and you may even attempt to convince yourself that you are falling for him. What a great deal. Now neither of you has to open up to real love. Is that the relationship you're really looking for? Or have you decided that you've reached a certain age, and this partnership may be as good as it gets? Ultimately, your true inner desire will rise up and resist. You will inevitably be faced with the decision to cut off the pseudo-romance and get on with your life.

The dreaded one-night stand is another option to satiate your sexual hunger. Can't find a great guy but want to feel good for one night? Sure, there are plenty of men who will take you up on the offer of a commitment-free romp in their bed. The evening will seem wonderful as you feel the intensity of the newness of the lover and make believe that there is an amazing connection between you. In the morning (if you stay that long), he makes breakfast and plans to see you again. You leave him with a smile that stays on your face until Thursday afternoon, when his phone call never comes. You can justify that you were getting your needs met, but somewhere deep in your mind your thoughts are telling you that you just weren't good enough, pretty enough, sexy enough, and so on, or he would have called. Worse, you can start beating yourself up for acting so slutty and vow never to do that again . . . until the next time.

If you don't honor yourself (including your body), no one else will. This is pretty obvious advice, but many single women fail to follow it. The modern woman should be able to have sex like a man does. Yes, sure . . . however, most women can't. Women have a wonderful gift of intimacy that reaches far beyond what a man could ever feel. You are a special, beautiful person, and why would you want to let someone into your body whom you have known for only a few hours?

You can pretend to put up a wall, but when you sleep with a man, everything changes. You start to care. Even if he is the most unattractive, dorky guy, you will care if he doesn't call after you sleep with him. Sure, you pretend that you don't, and even tell your friends that you don't, but you do. You may be convinced that you are indifferent, and you are adamantly disagreeing with me right now. If that is the case, you are probably not conscious of the effect that this behavior has on you. Whenever a woman gives a part of herself, as in sexual intimacy, she should expect to be honored. The only other possible reason for disrespecting her body is to use meaningless sex to continue to destroy her self-worth.

Lisa, a highly intelligent thirty-year-old journalist, had a history of going out to bars, having a few drinks, and sleeping with the man of the evening. She was extremely attractive and had no problem catching men. The next morning, she did the walk of shame, foggy-headed, in her clothes from the night before, back to her apartment. Some men hung around for a few weeks; others never called her at all. She tried to justify her actions by exclaiming that she was single and should be having a good time until Mr. Right showed up. Unfortunately, she tried to force every man whom she slept with into her husband-to-be photo album, without really paying attention to what she truly wanted in a partner.

She had not focused clearly on what she wanted or why she wanted a man. Her actions reflected her mind-set. When she started to work with me, she explained that she lived such a hectic lifestyle, with job deadlines and a full social life, that she never stopped to think about her behavior. She simply acted in the hopes that one man would stick.

She began to identify what she wanted and then get clear on what had sabotaged her goals in the past. She uncovered a false belief about not being lovable that stemmed from her childhood, when her father had completely ignored her. Her need for love was so intense that she would do anything to get approval, including push aside her own values. The belief that she was unlovable was also reinforced when the guys ultimately blew her off. By identifying the real issue, she started to find new ways to fill herself up with love. She stopped needing the attention of men to make herself feel good. Spending time with her fiction writing was a joyful replacement for her intoxicated evening flaunts. She took advantage of the alone time to really nurture herself.

She didn't become a hermit, and she still loved getting attention from men, but she didn't crave it anymore. She tried various places to meet people, such as art gallery openings and other social events that didn't revolve around drinking or a hookup. As she honored herself more, she stopped saying yes every time a guy invited her back to his place. The grasping feeling left, and she become more relaxed in social settings. She soon met an aspiring artist who absolutely adored her. By changing her thoughts and actions, she was able to get in alignment with the energy of true love, and she easily attracted her mate. Lisa's sexual promiscuity was a result of her need for attention, but some women have deeper roots of suffering that cause wanton behavior.

In certain extreme cases where women have been physically abused, sex becomes a familiar painful habit. Some women have disconnected themselves from the sexual act because as children they needed to do that to survive emotionally. Their defense was simply to shut out their hurt because they were powerless against the aggressor, but the pain still persisted. As adults, these women can become very promiscuous and often put themselves in abusive situations because the pain is so familiar to them. Their self-worth has been damaged, and they believe they do not deserve better. These harmful traumas remain deep and can often sabotage any attempt to be in a healthy, loving relationship. If this is the case with you, for maximum benefit you may want to seek counseling from a licensed professional or join a support group, in addition to doing the work in this book.

Legal Prostitution

A little twist to the oldest profession is when the woman pays the man for sex. Even though many people think that a woman can get sex anytime she wants, a gal might support her man financially to keep him in her life. Yes, believe it or not, there are some Janes out there, and you could be one of them!

Allison, a thirty-nine-year-old divorced lawyer, came to me brokenhearted. Her ten-year marriage had ended a year prior, and she had gotten involved with another man immediately after the divorce. She was a kind, compassionate woman who only wanted to do the right thing. She'd met a man online who was charming, handsome, and ten years younger than she. He absolutely adored her, and they fell in love immediately. She quickly invited him to move into her beautiful home, which she had retained as a part of her divorce settlement. She received a hefty maintenance check each month from her ex-husband, and her law practice provided a lavish income.

Her young boyfriend, Tom, had been in construction doing odd jobs but didn't have much to offer. He kept telling her that he wasn't materialistic and money didn't matter to him. You know where this is going, don't you? At first, he had some work, but his modest pay didn't compare to Allison's income, so he decided that his time would be better spent doing the landscaping and taking care of the house. He told her that he wanted to go back to school and finish his college degree. He had made big plans for them to build a life together and insisted that he needed a better education. Allison agreed to support him and pay his tuition because she wanted the best for him, and the money didn't matter to her. This went on for a few months until Tom dropped out. He claimed that school was too hard and that he just wasn't a "book guy." So, instead of getting a job, he stayed home. He then focused on some work-at-home Internet projects, but none of them ever amounted to anything. Most of the time, he sat on the couch and watched television all day while Allison worked.

She didn't mind this either, because he had dinner ready for her when she got home, and they had amazing sex. She liked taking care of her young boyfriend and kept justifying her actions by thinking that he would eventually find his way. Her resentment began when the dinners stopped, the frequency of sex decreased, and he became more irritable toward her. Bottling her feelings up inside, she didn't say anything to him because she was so afraid of his leaving her. Even though she was extremely successful financially, her self-worth crumbled in relationships, and her insecurity had been one of the reasons for her failed marriage.

When she came to me, she knew she had to change things but felt powerless to make a move. I asked her a question that I ask most of my clients who are in unhealthy relationships: "What are you getting out of this relationship?" Of course, the rationalizations flowed out easily, as if she'd rehearsed them in her head a million times, but then she paused.

"Well," she said, "I guess all I really get is good sex and not even as frequently as I want. I pay for all his expenses. He is like a male prostitute!" Then I asked the follow-up questions about the emotional cost to her of the good sex and asked her what she really wanted. She claimed to want a healthy relationship with mutual respect and love. I asked her why she was settling for a second-rate partnership. Her answer: "I didn't think what I wanted was available to me."

She discovered some core issues about not feeling good enough that created the neediness that eventually drove her ex-husband to have an affair. She was repeating the same insecure patterns with Tom, except that this time she was paying him to be with her so that he wouldn't dare leave. Deep in her mind, she believed that she needed to give something for a man to be with her; she wasn't enough on her own. Her ex didn't need the money; he had plenty of cash. With the younger poor guy she could control him, in a way. She created a situation that was too comfortable for him to ever want to leave.

After she cleared away her false beliefs on the subconscious level about not being good enough, she garnered enough courage to kick Tom out and start a new life on her own. She met her true love about six months later and is happily married again. Months after Tom left, she found out that he had been having an affair with a woman at the country club while Allison was working. His lack of interest in sex and his irritability made sense to her then. Even if you pay a man, your money does not guarantee that he will behave. Lesson: male prostitutes cannot be trusted.

The Comeback Kid

Some men simply will not go away. Even with all of your neuroses, quirks, and insecurities, there is always that one ex-lover who repeatedly shows up for more. This may not be true for all women, but for most women I've worked with there is one man from the past who resurfaces right at the time that the woman is most vulnerable. It's almost eerie how the old boyfriend can just feel you calling to him.

Anthony was one of those guys for my client Sheryl. At first, she came to me to get over Anthony. She cried during most of her first sessions, refusing to let go of the heartache, even though she realized that this man was an abusive, alcoholic womanizer. I told her that when she was finally over him, he would be on his knees begging for her to come back. She didn't believe me at first, but when she started to feel better and moved on with her life, sure enough, Mr. Wonderful called her, wanting to apologize and begging her to reconcile. She refused him initially, but after a few months of dating without finding Mr. Right, she slowly let him inch back into her life.

Justifying her actions by saying they were just friends, she continued with another month of her pseudo-romance until he was back to his old game. Mr. Wonderful turned into Mr. Abandonment . . . again. Once more, she was crying in my office, wondering what she'd done wrong. She was now angry at him *and* at herself.

If you have a comeback kid in your life, here are some ways to work around his advances so that you don't get caught in his false-love grip. Be aware that when you start to clear your mind and feel more confident, scores of men will approach you. Your old lovers will start calling and will want to be with you, too. As your attraction vibe increases, you will be irresistible! Know that you may still have a weak spot for those familiar boys, wanting to rekindle the old pattern of your unhealthy relationship. In some cases, the old love may have transformed himself as well, and you could possibly live happily ever after . . . but it's not likely. If your relationship didn't work before, why invite him back into your life? When you really want a relationship, you may be tempted to settle for a quick fix with a familiar man, instead of holding out for someone who meets your standards for Mr. Right.

There was a time in my late twenties when I was dating a guy named David. He was a great guy but just would not commit. I knew he wasn't dating anyone else, yet he always kept me at arm's length. When we got too close, he pulled away. He liked being in a relationship but not in a real one. When I attended social events with him, he always introduced me as his "friend." After a year of push and pull, I told him that I was dating other people. At first, he was fine with the idea. He cared about me but didn't want anything serious.

A few weeks after I declared my freedom, I met Jeff, who was an amazing, fun guy. We started dating each other while I was still seeing my "friend" David. I never told Jeff about David because our relationship was still very casual. Jeff and I weren't sleeping together, and I felt that I should keep my two worlds separate. Then I went away skiing for a weekend with Jeff, and he asked me to spend Valentine's Day with him that week. David confessed that he was extremely jealous of Jeff and wanted me to reconsider an exclusive relationship with him. I was thrilled. Even though Jeff treated me so nicely and we enjoyed each other, my heart was still hooked on David. So I broke it off with Jeff, who was very disappointed. Two weeks later, David was back to his old tricks of being uncommitted. What the heck had I done?

At this time I wasn't very confident. I felt comfortable with the familiarity of David, even though I really wanted a committed relationship. Jeff was obviously the better choice, but I succumbed to the cozy fickleness with David. My friends all thought I was crazy to dump Jeff. He was truly a great catch, and I just threw him back. Although he was one of the nicest guys I have ever dated, my mind was not in the right place back then to appreciate him. As I increased my confidence years later with self-hypnosis, I often wondered what would have happened if I had chosen Jeff. The story has a happy ending because I eventually met my true love, and I am sure Jeff is happily married now. As for David, he is still my friend.

You get to choose now what you want. That is why you created a clear vision of what you are looking for in a mate. You deserve more. You are worth more than a leftover relationship or someone you need to fix. The reason you gravitate to these familiar fellows is because they are predictable. You choose habitual pain, instead of reaching out to someone new who may just give you everything you ever wanted.

Now, the old boyfriend may simply be someone to keep you company while you continue to look around for your dream man. This is not the most effective way to realize your desires, because what you are saying to the universe is that you don't trust that your man is coming. You need to keep this other one around, just in case. Playing on both fields is not setting a very powerful intention. By clearing the space to make room for your new man to arrive, you create a feeling of trust and openness that the universe will provide.

Alicia was a forty-year-old woman who had never been married. When she first started her sessions with me, she had two guys in her back pocket, just in case she needed something to do. One lived in Florida and the other lived in New York, while she lived in Denver. The situation was very convenient, with no strings attached and no expectations, and she thought that she could handle the casual affairs. She had flight benefits because her friends worked for the airlines, so she was always able to jump on a flight and pay only the taxes. Her setup was very convenient. She wanted a committed relationship, however, and she knew the two men were not looking for anything serious.

As she increased her self-worth, she grew tired of the superficial buddies and ended both relationships. She seemed to always have men around but was now able to weed out the ones who were only looking to have fun. When she finally stood her ground and stopped playing with temporary men, she met her future husband within a few weeks.

Why Settle for Second Best?

Your deep mind is always working to keep your habits going. Whether the tendency is biting your fingernails or dating Mr. Wrongs, it's tough to let go of old habits. Your subconscious mind keeps you indulging in past behavior by rationalizing your actions.

Women use many justifications when they are settling. If you have ever had a meaningless fling, some of these may sound familiar to you. Here are my top twenty excuses for dating Mr. Right Now:

1. All the good men are taken.
2. I don't deserve more.
3. I can keep my heart and emotions separate from sex.
4. I want to have a good time while I am single.
5. He treats me well.
6. He gets along well with my family and friends.
7. He may turn into Mr. Right one day.

8. If I spend enough time with him, he will eventually fall in love with me.

9. I like sex and need to have it on a regular basis.

10. I am not hurting anybody.

11. We have an agreement.

12. What's wrong with having a good time?

13. I hate to be lonely.

14. All of my friends are married, and I need someone to spend time with.

15. I crave affection.

16. I am still dating other men, so what's the problem?

17. We use protection.

18. He treats me better than any man before him.

19. He really cares about me, and I like that.

20. I am only going to sleep with him until I meet the right guy.

Sound familiar? If not, maybe you have heard one of those excuses from your girlfriends. Your subconscious is so clever. If you find pleasure in something, the deep mind will continue to repeat the pattern and convince you that you are doing the right thing. Because you really want to date Mr. Right Now, you will listen to the voice in your head that says, "Yes, this is good, keep doing this." The problem is that your deep mind is not rational. As I mentioned many times previously, your inner mind simply follows patterns. If you do *that* and as a result you feel good, the mind wants to keep doing *that*.

Most of the time, Mr. Right Now causes you pain, so you may be wondering why your deep mind would push you to undergo more suffering. This is the tricky part. Your deep mind is so intelligent, it can determine which pain is worse, and it drives you to the *lesser pain*. Look at the following scenarios. One, you are desperate and lonely and feel sad without a man. Two, you are desperate and lonely; you momentarily feel good around your temporary man, and then he leaves and you feel sad again. Hmmm . . . your inner mind will chose the latter scenario because at least you get a little momentary joy, even if the uplift is minimal. Your mind will drive you back to the second scenario with justifications and excuses until you come up with a *new* option.

You don't have to wait until you experience a better situation for your subconscious to move toward; you can create a new one with the power of your imagination. Using hypnosis to get into the habit of feeling good about yourself, whether you are alone or with a man, will make you invincible in the dating world. You can teach your inner mind anything. Flexibility is the beauty of your subconscious. Remember that you are operating primarily on your default mental programs, so grab the wheel and start driving in a new direction.

The following exercise is a great way to visualize cutting away the ties to the men of your past and refocus your energy on creating a new future. If you have a temporary man in your life now, this is an effective method of releasing him and making yourself available for the right person. You can also cut ties from anyone who is not in your life but who still may have an emotional connection with you that makes you uneasy.

SELF-HYPNOSIS

Cutting Ties

Be sure to read through the entire exercise before you start.

Find a comfortable place to relax, and use your favorite hypnotic-induction technique. Suggestions for inductions: progressive relaxation or walking down a hallway and opening a door to a peaceful place.

Now that you are relaxed, step out into a beautiful place. It can be anywhere you like—a beach, a mountain meadow, a forest, a garden, and so on.

Take in all of the sights, smells, and sounds. Really get connected to what's around you and bring up your "good feeling," the specific one that you decided on in the Good Feeling exercise. If you have a color surrounding this feeling, allow the color to move through your body and out three to six feet around you. Feel yourself completed enveloped in this wonderful emotion and energy.

First, ask your subconscious mind whether there are any men in your life whom you need to clear today, and wait to see who shows up. (If you have a difficult time visualizing anyone, try to simply sense a face or a feeling.)

If you like, you can have a small dialogue with him and tell him good-bye. You are not going to cut away from the love, only from the unhealthy attachment that you both share. You can set him free. Now imagine dark cords that attach you to him like energetic strings or ropes, and bring in a beautiful golden sword to cut through the cord and disconnect the bond. Allow the broken cords to dissolve into the sky, far away from both of you.

In the places where the cords were attached, imagine a healing salve coming in to repair the damage that his attachment has caused you. Allow him to dissolve from your mind and your sight.

(If necessary, you can repeat this process with as many men as you like until you are done clearing.)

Think of a time in your life when you felt safe and secure. Bring in a loving shower of light to cleanse your body and mind of any remaining energy that may be lingering from that relationship. Now imagine that beautiful light filling in any gaps that were made when the strings were present. (Pause . . . allow enough time for the energy from these relationships to clear.)

When you feel that the release is complete, set the intention that this light creates a shield of protection against any man who does not have the qualities that you seek. The field is permeable enough to let love pass in and out. Imagine the energy going out into the world, announcing that you are free and ready to receive real love.

(Option: you can invite your future love into the visualization if you want to.)

Count up to five and open your eyes.

Suggestions

Feel free to say these to yourself before you count up to five, if you'd like.

I allow only loving, committed men in my life.

I respect myself and know that this level of respect is shown by the men I attract.

I honor my body and keep it from emotional and physical harm.

I surround myself with people who make me feel good about myself.

I know I deserve a good relationship.

I allow honest, caring men into my life.

I nurture myself and trust my judgment.

I have a clear vision of the healthy relationship I am drawing to me now.

I avoid men who do not meet my criteria for a good partnership.

I recognize the good guys and attract them continually.

The Cutting Ties exercise is wonderful for clearing out old energy to make room for your new man. You can do this visualization over and over until you have cleared away all of the men from your past who might be floating around in your subconscious, preventing the flow of love toward you.

Warning!

Cutting ties sometimes results in unwanted phone calls from the person you worked with in the session! Be prepared. Don't fall for his excuses, apologies, and promises to change. When you become empowered, you become *more attractive*. Your heart may be soft for the old familiar love, but focus on what you want. If you really want a healthy relationship, make a commitment to yourself to move on. Stand strong and don't give him *any* leeway to edge his way back into your heart. Don't allow yourself to be manipulated into a second-rate relationship again. This could be a way that the universe is testing you to see whether you are really ready. Remember, you deserve so much more!

Reinforcing Your Experience

Continue with your daily self-hypnosis and adjust your suggestions as you like. If an old love resurfaces who is hard to resist, do the Cutting Ties exercise again. Make sure that you let go of all of the attachments to him so that you can be free. Sense and notice any stubborn deep roots. If you still have trouble with removing the core belief, ask the energy what it needs to feel better, and give yourself that feeling. Once you experience a more pleasant feeling, the roots should become loose and melt away. You have the choice about what you want to keep and let go. You are in control.

10

Just Do It:
The Nonaction Trap

Action expresses priorities.

—Mahatma Gandhi

One of the biggest pitfalls that prevents love from entering your life is if you stay out of action. Are you sick of the dating game and want to give up, or are you afraid to even put yourself out there? Just like any conditioned behavior, nonaction can be a pattern that you relive repeatedly, but it often goes unnoticed because you believe you are not *doing* anything.

Even in stillness, you are always doing something. Your body is made up of energy, both physical and mental, that never ceases during the course of your life. When you sit on a bus or relax on the couch, you are in motion. Some actions are swift and noticeable, and others very subtle. The act of doing nothing is something. Everything you do, whether actively or passively, sends a signal to your subconscious mind about what you really want. Just because you are older now and beyond your formative years doesn't mean that your subconscious has stopped taking notes. Your subconscious mind is always learning about you and upgrading your "software."

So when you are lazy about improving your dating life, nothing happens. Even though your mind has the ability to draw the right person to you, this cannot happen too easily if you never leave the house. It is your actions that will help you *meet* him. In rare cases, a woman who avoids taking action might get a date with a delivery man who comes to the door. My friend Wendy once dated her UPS guy. The romance didn't last very long, but she got special treatment with her deliveries during their short-lived romance. The point is that your opportunities to meet someone greatly increase when you go places that men frequent. If you want a relationship but are not taking any steps to change your single status, there is an obstruction in your subconscious mind about attracting love.

The rationale for your inaction will sound very reasonable and logical. You have many inner personalities whose main job is to figure out how to talk you out of moving away from your comfort zone. These inner voices come in many different guises. Maybe you have noticed them lurking in your mind. I put them into five categories so that you can easily identify the nemesis of your love life and the excuses she gives you:

1. *Procrastinator*. I'll start dating next month, next year, when I lose weight, when I fix myself, when my kids grow up, and so on.
2. *Worrier*. I'm afraid of rejection. Online dating is dangerous. I am afraid of someone raping, kidnapping, or killing me.
3. *Skeptic*. There is no use in trying. There is no one out there for me. I will never meet anyone.
4. *Bitch*. Men suck. Guys are not worth my time. Stay away!
5. *Beginner*. I don't know the first thing about dating, and I am not ready to put myself out there.

The Procrastinator

With every change you have to make in life, you ultimately face the procrastinator. The procrastinator acts like your friend because she pretends to agree with your desire (such as going out on a date), but cunningly convinces you that this simply is not the right time. Is there ever a perfect time for anything? No matter how much you plan, you always end up looking back and wishing your choices could be different. The reason the procrastinator is so effective is that she works under the premise that there is never a good time, so you never take action. Her ultimate goal is to keep you stuck. When one excuse wears off, another reason will conveniently pop up. To break the cycle, you must stop believing that sometime in the future is a better time than now to make changes in your life.

The procrastinator will use anything, even this book, to keep you from moving forward. Have you thought, Maybe I shouldn't date until I finish this book and do all of the exercises? It sounds reasonable that you want to make sure your mind is in the right place for love before you venture out into the world of dating again. But this is only a clever justification. You should go out and enjoy all of the wonderful changes you experience during this process. And I've got a secret for you: when you are finished with this book, you still won't have a perfect mind. Your personal development is an ongoing, lifelong process.

By playing on the field of life (instead of watching from the bleachers), you are fully engaged and open to new opportunities. You open the door to love and welcome that special someone in. The specific action you take is irrelevant; what matters is your intention to put yourself out in the world and explore. One client, who had been coming to me for about six months to work on gaining confidence after a terrible divorce, finally broke away from an intermittent relationship and decided to join a dating service. Before she went on her first date from the service, friends introduced her to a single man who became her next long-term love. All that was necessary was that she simply make changes that were in alignment with what she wanted. Clearing out the old relationship and joining the service generated an opening in her life to let this new man in. I hear stories like this from my clients all the time.

Recognizing and discounting the procrastinator in your thoughts can propel you forward and can drive you to your dream man. Yet although the procrastinator is subtle in her disguise, a deeper layer of avoidance can be created by the worrier, whose techniques are blatantly obvious attempts to keep you from acting.

The Worrier

Do you spend time obsessing over Internet fraud, date rape, or the crime statistics in your town? Or do you worry about rejection, a common fear? The world can sometimes be a dangerous place, of course, but if everyone stayed inside hiding from all of the bad people, no one would ever meet! I don't endorse taking risks like going to a bad neighborhood at night or having a stranger pick you up at your house for a first date. You should always use common sense and take precautions when you go out socially. The voice of the worrier, however, has *unreasonable* ideas of danger that prevent you from seeking opportunities to find love. This voice warns you that if you take action, something terrible will happen.

When you are fearful, your mind immediately thinks you are going to die. Whether you are worried about being rejected or being killed, the stressful "fight or flight" response in your body is the same, and the worrier's voice will make every effort to avert this perceived danger. Everyone has experienced rejection in one way or another, and sometimes the pain does make you feel as if you are going to die. As if someone took away your life raft and you are floating in a dangerous ocean of uncertainty. A certain man's approval is what kept you afloat, and without his acknowledgment, you feel as if you are drowning.

The idea of sinking and losing your ability to breathe is not a pleasant experience, so why take the risk? Why put yourself out there in the world of dangerous men, to have them steal away what little self-worth you have left? This is how the worrier thinks, always identifying with the worst-case scenario.

The worrier will exaggerate everything to make the outcome seem so bad that you avoid action altogether. If you dissect the story that you are telling yourself, you will realize that most of the thoughts are simply designed to keep you from your true love. Like a car salesman who doesn't want you to walk away, the worrier will make her case and bend the truth so that she gets what she wants. Remember that this aspect of your mind is not bad or evil; the worrier thinks she is protecting you. She has your best interests in mind (unlike some car salesmen).

In order to overcome a fear, you must face the threat directly. Find ways to soothe the worrier inside of you. Understand what she is really afraid of and ease her trepidation. Elaine, a fifty-year-old dental hygienist, came to me after a number of bad breakups. She knew the men she'd broken up with weren't her perfect match, but she still could not stand the rejection. She stopped dating and socializing to protect herself from any future pain. Here's how our dialogue went:

Me: What are you really afraid of?

Elaine: Heartache.

Me: Why is the heartache so scary?

Elaine: Because it feels so uncomfortable.

Me: Can you describe what this uncomfortable feeling means to you?

Elaine: It means that I am no good, and every time someone rejects me, that is what I feel, and I hate to feel that way so I don't want to put myself out there again.

Me: So you are rejecting them first before they have the chance to get to you?

Elaine: (pause) I guess.

Me: So you want to be in control of the rejection and protect yourself from that awful feeling?

Elaine: Yes.

Me: Would you be open to another way of doing that and still being able to date and have fun?

Elaine: Is it possible?

Me: To get back in control, change the story in your mind about what the rejection means.

Elaine: How could it mean anything else except that I am no good?

Me: Have you ever rejected anyone?

Elaine: Well . . . I am sure at some point.

Me: Did you reject them because they were no good?

Elaine: Most of the time it was because I did not feel a connection with them.

Me: Does that make them no good, unlovable?

Elaine: No, because it's only my personal opinion.

Me: So why do you assume their rejection means what you made up in your mind?

Elaine: Because that is what I always do. It's how I see myself.

Me: Imagine if you saw yourself differently. How would you want to see yourself?

Elaine: Beautiful, smart, fun to be around, sexy. Is that ridiculous?

Me: Not at all. If you felt beautiful, smart, fun to be around, and sexy and someone still rejected you, what would you think?

Elaine: His loss!

Me: Exactly. His rejection has nothing to do with how he thinks; it's how *you* think.

Elaine: So I could make up anything?

Me: Elaine, you have been making up things your whole life.

By default, you may find it easier to determine that a rejection or a breakup is terrible than to make the experience mean something more positive or even neutral. The only difference is in how you decide to look at the situation. In relationships, women tend to take negative responses from men more personally. Why does the rejection always have to be about you? You have no idea what is going through the man's mind, what his current relationship status is, or whether he is even capable of being a good partner. Women put the men whom they date up on pedestals before the guys have earned that status.

My friend Darlene's story illustrates this. She met Ryan when she was in her twenties and thought he was top-notch. They attended personal-development training together, and she looked up to him as someone who had it all together. When he asked her out on a date, she was thrilled, hoping that she would measure up to his standards. They had a great time, but after their date, she never heard from him again. She took years to get over this. All of her beliefs about not being good enough rose to the surface, and she always wondered what she had done that was so wrong for Ryan never to call her again.

About ten years went by, and she ran into a mutual friend who had taken the same training course. She asked her friend about Ryan and was surprised at what he said. Ryan's story about their date was completely opposite of Darlene's impression. He'd told this mutual friend that he was so excited about Darlene and their amazing date. He thought that she was "the one," but he wasn't ready for her, and he ran away. So Darlene had wasted all of those years tearing herself apart because she believed that he'd rejected her because she wasn't good enough. The point I'm trying to make is that you just never know what is going on with another person. You have the power to decide what tale you will make up about any circumstance.

The story you create is always the same by default. If your core belief is that you aren't good enough, you will think that every negative situation that occurs in your life is because you aren't good enough. As you work with your mind to change your deep beliefs to more supportive ideas, your mind's story line begins to change, and your reaction to external events becomes less painful.

Imagine the freedom you would have to go on a date and never feel rejected, even when a man does not call back. By easily exclaiming, "His loss," you get to build up courage to love yourself more and take more chances when meeting new people. The best way to approach dating is as if it's a cold call in sales. You know you aren't going to get a yes every time, but each no is simply one no closer to Mr. Right. The important element is not the person's response but that you are out there making yourself available to meet your guy. Did you know that I have a four-letter word for men who do not love and adore me? N-E-X-T!

Along with the fear of rejection is a more intense worry: social anxiety. I have worked with many clients who claim that their anxiousness is caused by crowds or their shyness. What they really are afraid of is people not liking them. Feeling insecure about themselves, they shrink in the corner at parties and blend in with the curtains. When introduced to new people, they often get tongue-tied, sweaty palms, and panic feelings in their chest. Who would enjoy an evening out if that happened every time? They have always preferred simply to stay home.

The worrier is again in action. Afraid of embarrassment, this part of your mind always talks you out of attending any social engagement and even convinces you that you aren't feeling well about thirty minutes prior to your leaving. You retreat, stay home, and hear from your friends the next day about the fun they had at the party. Again, it's up to you to decide what other people think about you. You cannot hear their thoughts, so why be so afraid?

Most people with social anxiety experienced an early childhood event in which they were embarrassed in front of other people. The experience was so emotionally painful that the subconscious mind learned that social situations are scary and dangerous. The subconscious pulls out all of its excuses to keep you from attending the gathering, including dramatic physical reactions. The stronger the initial emotional event was, the greater the intensity of the anxiety that you experience in the present.

With self-hypnosis, you can relieve this anxiousness almost immediately. Make sure that you go back to chapter 7 to do the Seven-Step Feeling exercise and work with the fear. All feelings are valid and should be addressed. The worst thing you can do is try to numb the feeling with drugs or alcohol or succumb to the emotion and stay home. Once you transform the worrier into a powerful presence inside, you will begin to be more comfortable out in the dating world. Yet even as the worrier uses intense feeling to make you retreat from life, the skeptic uses your intellect and doubt to keep you stuck.

The Skeptic

The part of your mind that tells you to give up before you even begin is the skeptic. Why bother? What's the use? There is no one out there for me anyway. You may have inherited the doubting voice from someone you grew up with, such as one of your parents, sibling, or an other relative. Usually, the skeptic appears when you reach for your dreams and someone says you will never attain your goals.

I remember a conversation I had with my junior high friends on the way to the mall when I was twelve. We were talking about who would be the first to get married and the pecking order of the group following the first one. They all decided that I would be the last. Well, their prediction actually turned out to be right. Coupled with all of my other negative junior high experiences with boys, I held the doubt that I would ever find true love. These persona-forming events got firmly embedded in my subconscious mind and created my dating destiny until I changed it. The good news is that I kept taking action to avoid my lonely fate. Some women succumb to the doubt and don't even try.

There are skeptics everywhere: the naysayers at the office, the critical mother, or the evening news guy. The most powerful skeptic is inside you, and if you let her rule, she will steal your hopes and dreams and leave you disenchanted. What the skeptic is really doing is also keeping you safe from disappointment, just as others around you have done.

Remember when you were little and people asked what you wanted to be when you grew up? You may have said, "An astronaut," "The president," or "A Broadway star." Instead of encouraging you, they might have convinced you to aim for more realistic goals, such as being a secretary or a bookkeeper. What cynics did you face when you reached a certain age and still had not met Mr. Right? Have family members made comments about the dwindling chances of getting married as you age? Or, how about your single girlfriends? Do they try to convince you to give up on your search for love? Do they complain about being single all the time? Are your coupled friends telling you that marriage is overrated and you are better off being single?

People doubt because they fear hope. They believe that if they have hope, they will be disappointed. They find safety in expecting the worst. Unfortunately, what you expect tends to happen. If you allow the cynical voice to take over your life, you will always get what you expect—not much.

Christina had had enough. She was closing in on forty, with no husband-to-be in sight. She tried to think positively and visualize her man coming, but she always felt skeptical about everything she did to get her mind in the right place. After her last "almost the one" romance fell apart, she decided that she was finished. Digging in her heels, she was taking herself off the market. She told me, "Marriage isn't going to happen, so why do I even try?"

Many single women go through a phase in which they simply want to give up. Sometimes it can be good for them to let go of all that tension in trying to meet a man. The release allows them to relax and create an opening to let love in. For others, the break lasts way too long and they become despondent. When this occurs, action stops. They pull their online profiles, stop going out with friends, and resign themselves to a lifetime of being alone. Sometimes when people are desperate for love, they become extremists. They are highly focused on finding "the one" for a while and then they totally lose faith. Feeling like failures, they allow the skeptic to take control.

There were many times when I felt like giving up. Because I had no evidence except my visualizations to support my dream of a happy relationship, doubts crept into my mind. Yet around the same time, I had the urge to join a dating service. One day later, I spoke to my soon-to-be mate, and my love life completely changed. The point is that you never know what tomorrow could bring. Even if you've had a thousand lonely days, the next one could be the day that he arrives. The skeptic will try to persuade you to give up, but, as you will discover in the next section, the bitch takes her case to a whole new level.

The Bitch

Have you heard your inner bitch? She is angry and frustrated with your dating life. She's really pissed. She hates men, is frustrated with society, and wants you to stay away from anything that seems happy and romantic. She really gets annoyed during the holidays and especially when one of her friends announces an engagement or a pregnancy. She is not happy for anyone until she gets what she wants.

Closely related to the skeptic, the bitch takes it up a few notches on sarcasm and energy. She doesn't passively complain but actively proclaims that life is not fair. She is so mad that her heart is closed and she won't let anyone in. She gave up on dating a long time ago and now just barks at people for having children in an overpopulated world or throwing their money away on Hallmark holidays.

The inner bitch doesn't want to have fun and will do everything in her power to make you miserable and hopeless. She will devise a plethora of justifications for not taking action in your dating life. If you do and fail, she will be the first one to chew you out. Oh, she's tough.

The bitchy girl just needs a little love. She has put up a wall to keep everyone out because she really feels vulnerable and scared. The next time this girl's voice shows up in your mind, simply give her a hug and let her know that she is safe. The more you can calm her pain, the less she'll get in the way of your taking action toward meeting Mr. Wonderful. The bitch may be loud, but at least she has some passion. Redirect her fervor to shift yourself into action; this can help you move beyond your comfort zone.

The Beginner

You have read stories up to this point of women who have been in relationships, but I know that some of you out there have little or no experience in the romance department. Dating wisdom doesn't always come with age. Some people go through their entire adult lives dating only their high school sweethearts-turned-husbands. When they get divorced twenty years later or their spouses pass on, they are thrust into the dating scene without instructions. These women (and men) come to me for advice because they don't know how to date. Inexperience can be an obstacle to building the courage to take action.

Being in a relationship is much different from dating, in certain ways. Also, courtship twenty years ago was very different than it is today. We are now in a time when online dating, cell phones, and text messages are thrown into the romance mix. Wondering how the modern dating world works, beginners can feel out of place and out of touch.

Other late bloomers come to me because they have never been in a relationship at all. Some are in their twenties and have never kissed a man, and others are virgins in their forties and fifties.

These singles want to date but feel uncomfortable about their history. They are embarrassed, and they feel abnormal, disconnected from regular society.

No matter what your history is, your past does not define you. Whether you slept with hundreds of men or are a virgin at forty, what you did (or did not do) in the past is inconsequential. Your life experiences are merely a string of stories that don't exist anymore, outside of your memories and imagination. You can begin today with a fresh perspective.

Morgan, a twenty-five-year-old computer programmer, wanted to believe that love was possible for her, but she felt very unprepared for dating. She considered herself a freak for being a virgin at her age, and she'd never had the experience of kissing a man. She wondered what guys would think about her lack of experience. She withdrew into herself so much that she was afraid to let herself out. Through self-hypnosis, she got to practice what it was like to be on a date by visualizing being held and loved by a man. She used romantic movie scenes as a reference point, and this helped her tremendously. It took a while, but she finally began to change her outlook and believe that she could attract romance into her life.

I coached her to make friends with men first. I encouraged her to join a class or a group in something she was interested in, to allow her inner social butterfly out of the cocoon. After a few months, she became interested in a man in her writing class. He was pretty shy as well but mustered up the courage to ask her out. Her very first date! She eventually dated a few different men over the next year until she found one whom she really liked. Morgan was surprised at how easily she came out of her shell. Her prior fears were unwarranted as she took action and used self-hypnosis, and her romantic life blossomed.

No matter what your voice tells you, learn to listen to your heart. If you truly want a relationship, pay attention to the voice that cheers you on, instead of to the one that knocks you down. If you find yourself resistant in taking action, you could do the following hypnosis sessions to remove the blocks in your inner mind.

SELF-HYPNOSIS

The Ball and Chain

Be sure to read through the entire exercise before you start.

Find a comfortable place to relax, and use your favorite hypnotic-induction technique. Suggestions for inductions: progressive relaxation or counting down from fifteen to one and take deep, relaxing breaths.

Now that you are relaxed, step out into a mountain meadow. Take in all of the sights, smells, and sounds. Really get connected to the natural beauty around you. As you start to walk through the meadow, you see a sign ahead marking a new road that says, "The Man of My Dreams." While you look at the sign, feel the resistance inside yourself as you think about taking action . . . going down that road. Notice that you cannot move toward the road because something is holding you back; you feel stuck where you are standing. Get in touch with the feeling of resistance.

When you feel your resistance, look down at one of your legs and see that there is a ball and chain attached to your leg with a shackle. The ball and chain represent all of those subconscious reasons for your inaction. Take a good look at the ball and see an image, a word, or a phrase that represents the block. Take your time to notice what is really holding you back.

Ask your inner mind whether it would be all right if you released the block now, for your highest good. Wait for a definitive answer. If it is yes, continue on. (If it is no, explain to that part of yourself that you will keep it safe and promise to make sure that it is well taken care of. Ask again for permission to release; you can start surrounding yourself in your "good feeling" for support and keep the dialogue with that resisting part until you understand the resistance and you get a clear yes.)

If the answer is yes, bring up your "good feeling" and color and surround the ball and chain with the color to dissolve it. Release yourself from this block, once and for all.

Now scan your body and see whether there is any remnant of that block still within your body. If so, make the block a dark cloud and release it. Fill yourself up with your "good feeling" and dissolve any remaining dark spots until you feel completely clear. (Pause.)

Now that you are clear, imagine that you can easily walk toward the road that leads to the man of your dreams. Fill yourself with great anticipation of someone wonderful coming into your life. It is all right if you don't know where the road leads; just keep holding the faith that you will be guided in the right direction. If it helps, you can imagine angels or spiritual helpers or guides taking your hand and showing you the way.

(Option: Here you can imagine greeting your future mate at the end of the road and telling him that you are ready for him. When you have finished the conversation with him, you can bring the good feelings back with you.)

Count up to five and open your eyes.

Suggestions

Feel free to say these to yourself before you count up to five, if you'd like.

I take action every day toward my goals.

When I am taking action, I feel empowered and confident.

I know the steps I need to take to meet my true love.

I perform each act in a successful manner with my clear vision in my mind.

With each action I take, I feel as if I have already attracted my man to me.

I listen to internal nudges and act on them immediately.

I find my way around all obstacles and continue to move forward.

My mind is always thinking toward my goal and feeling good about meeting my true love.

I know that with every action, I am closer and closer to meeting my mate.

I continue to take steady action with unwavering faith.

Now that you have cleared the block that kept you from moving forward, you can make some plans. Just as with any endeavor, having a good plan is a great foundation for getting what you want. Making a plan may seem a little cold and unromantic, but a plan is the perfect tool if you have trouble focusing or staying on course in your dating life.

Journaling

The Action Plan

Open to a fresh page in your journal and brainstorm a list of activities that you'd like to do or places you'd like to visit. After you make your list, take a highlighter and mark any activities and places that you believe your potential romantic partner may be interested in as well. Take a fresh page and then prioritize them according to importance and highest interest.

When you really analyze what you like, you will probably realize that many of your favorite activities may occur in a place where you might meet a potential partner. Now, starting with the interest that is on the top of your list (your favorite), create a plan for when you will take part in the activity. Many people like to do various things but seldom find the time to do them. Choose a target date and commit to taking up this hobby or pursuing this activity by that date (or you can make it daily or weekly, if you like, instead of it being a onetime event). Indicate any steps you'll need to take to do this activity or reach the target date. Here's an example of how such a plan may look, but feel free to design your own personal plan in a way that works best for you.

Action Plan

Activity/Goal: Attend art lectures once a month

Target Date: May 1

Steps to Take

    Research art museums

    Get schedule of lectures at chosen museum

    Attend first lecture

Action Plan

Activity/Goal: Take an acting class

Target Date: Begin class by June 1

Steps to Take

    Research acting schools

    Call and/or visit various schools

    Sign up for a class

    Attend first class

Review your action plan often to make sure you are on task. If you follow your plan, amazing things will happen. Developing a plan helps solidify your strong desire, and your state of readiness is communicated to the creative forces around you. You may not meet your romantic partner in the place that you expect, but setting the intention and taking action by performing the steps creates motion and eventually brings to you what you want. If you put off this task or find that you are not willing to go to new places, ask yourself whether you are really serious about finding the love of your life. Any hesitation could indicate another subconscious block that is still working against your will. Repeat the Ball and Chain exercise or any of the other self-hypnosis exercises in this book to help you release the inner saboteur so that you can move on and find love.

Mindful Actions

A simple act can speak volumes to the universe. Consistent action will ensure that a flow of love opportunities comes toward you. Mindful action increases the power of intention tenfold. By aligning your thoughts and actions, you create a powerful elixir that makes you unstoppable in your quest for true love.

When you do repetitive tasks, your mind often gets distracted, thinking of other things. You automatically ride the thoughts that rise up to the surface from your deep mind. While making dinner, you could be thinking about your day at the office, or you might obsess over a previous conversation with a good friend while you are shopping at the mall. The mind is conditioned to be anywhere but right here, right now. If you don't take control of your thoughts and feelings, you are missing out on the most powerful way to materialize your new love.

To take back the reins of your thinking, it is essential to stay fully in the present moment. The first objective is to refrain from negative thinking in general. Keep your mind focused on what you want to ensure your success. The second objective is to perform supportive actions while your mind is thinking about what you want. The third objective is to incorporate feeling into the mix. Intense, empowered feelings and thoughts and clear actions can increase the strength of your manifestation by having all of these elements in sync simultaneously.

Mindful Online Dating

Writing your profile. You dilute your intentions if you are writing your online profile and thinking, No one is going to like me, or, There are probably only jerks on this site, but what the heck? When you write your personal description online, make sure that you really feel those good qualities in yourself, and imagine your true love responding, so happy to finally find you. When I wrote my profile for the dating service, I put my hands over the finished copy and envisioned that the paper was surrounded with light. If you are using a computer, put your hands on the monitor and send the words a positive vibration.

Between your words, there is a silent space that holds energy. If you are writing words that you don't believe, men will be able to feel the deception. They know when you are lying, pretending, and insecure. They can sense your lack of confidence. Even if you post the most beautiful picture to your profile, if your energy creates an impression that you are down and discouraged, you will always attract the men who disappoint you.

E-mail communication. When responding to e-mails, keep your mind focused on being in love. Surround your e-mails with loving energy as if you are sending a little fairy dust along with your message. Even if your target does not ultimately make the cut, he will still benefit from receiving loving thoughts. Remember the energy between your words in every message that you send. Men can sense you from miles away.

Match selection. Don't overscrutinize your suitors. Allow each of them an opportunity to prove that he is the right fit. Remain upbeat and positive, even if you get some rejections. This is just one less guy you have to deal with to reach your dream man. Use your intuition before giving out your phone number or scheduling a meeting.

Mindful Social Networking

Before you attend a party or an event where there will be single men, make a mental and/or physical list of all of your good qualities. Think about how lucky someone would be to have you in his life. Focus on three of your best qualities, and keep them in the forefront of your mind the entire time. Really feel that "good feeling" (imagine being surrounded by your "good feeling" color) during the evening.

When speaking to a potential love interest, keep your mind focused on how good you feel about yourself. This may sound a little egotistical, but if you had problems with self-esteem before reading this book, I am sure you won't be putting yourself over the top just yet. Smile and be open to discovering what he has to offer you. Remember, *you* get to choose whom you allow into your life.

Your Mind on a First Date

When you go out on a date with someone new, be open to whatever the man has to offer. Keep your expectations limited to that evening. Have a good time and enjoy the company of another person without being overly eager. Avoid acting desperate or trying to figure out whether he is Mr. Right, and don't discard him before you learn more about him. Get to know the person in front of you without focusing on the prospect of future dates or spending your lives together. Give him the space to show you who he is, and you will be less anxious to make him fit into your friend/lover/nobody filing system.

If your mind is not present with the moment, he will feel that you are sizing him up. You will also sense whether he is doing the same to you. By relaxing into whatever arises out of your date, you can be more comfortable being yourself. You won't put him into the position of being on guard and pretending to be someone else just to impress you. Relax and reduce the pressure by allowing the evening to unfold naturally.

Every date you have occurs exclusively in your mind. The food, the atmosphere, and the conversation have little effect on your destiny together, compared to what you both are thinking. Clear your mind, leave your past stuff at home, and be open to experiencing a new person without conditions, expectations, or those darn dating rules. He will feel your lightness of spirit, and that will allow him to be his best self as well.

Tips for Successful Dating

After doing self-hypnosis, you will undoubtedly see a difference in your level of confidence. If you have never had second dates before, be assured that you will get asked out again and again. Whether you are a beginner or someone who has not had much experience in healthy dating, this ritual may be new for you. You may be uncertain about how to act, so I have set down some tips to help you keep your mind in check as the relationship develops.

There's no rush. No matter how excited you are about your new love interest, don't rush into a commitment too quickly. Use your intuition to sense the right time to get closer, physically and sexually. Most women who have been single for a long time get overly zealous, and they latch onto the first guy who shows them interest. They scrutinize their new guy's every move and even ask him bluntly whether he is in the relationship for the long haul. If you feel overwhelming urges to act like this, realize that it's coming from a sense of lack, of feeling unworthy, and use some of the self-hypnosis techniques to transform these emotions. A woman who is certain that she is worthy of being loved is confident enough to wait, instead of pushing for a premature commitment from a man.

Focus on being successful. When you like someone, tension can build up inside you because you feel on guard, afraid to make any mistakes. Your subconscious will attempt to remind you of all of your past dating blunders, but you are the one who decides what your future holds. You are now a more confident person, and you can turn the tide of your dating destiny by focusing on success.

Don't turn him into a god. Don't put your new love interest on a pedestal. He is not your god or your savior. He is only a man. Until he can prove over time that he is worthy of you, let him remain with the rest of the commoners in the dating pool. By putting him above you, you automatically place yourself below him. Keep your mind focused on believing that *you* are the prize. You are a great catch, and he should be lucky to have found you.

Don't take rejection too personally. Unfortunately, dating sometimes results in the big blow-off. Everyone has experienced this awful event at least once in his or her dating life. If your new man decides not to return your calls after a few dates, let him go and move on. The worst thing you can do is to feel bad about yourself and let this one experience destroy your newfound confidence. You have no idea why he didn't call, and your mind will make up stories based on your belief system. If you find that you are taking rejection too personally, listen to a confidence-building hypnosis program or do your own self-hypnosis exercise to get your mind back on track.

Reinforcing Your Experience

Continue with daily self-hypnosis to increase your confidence about, and motivation for, dating. Perform at least one action per day that will lead to your possibly meeting your man. Even small actions count (such as researching dating sites). As you put your toes into the water, you'll see that the temperature isn't so bad, and hopefully you'll find yourself diving into full-action dating!

PART THREE

Staying in Your Lane of Love: Keeping the Faith

Without faith, nothing is possible. With it, nothing is impossible.

—Mary McLeod Bethune

After clearing your mind of false core beliefs and aligning your actions and emotions with meeting Mr. Right, you will also need to have unwavering faith. By expecting success, you create an unbreakable link connecting your thoughts, your feelings, and your actions in order to attract your true love. This section discusses how to release the beliefs that destroy your faith so that all of your efforts are in sync. Your mind holds the idea, your actions reaffirm your commitment, and your faith allows your spirit to interact with the energies of creation.

11

Dancing with the Green-Eyed Monster

If you judge people, you have no time to love them.
—Mother Teresa

Do you walk into a room and compare yourself to everyone around you to determine who is thinner, dressed more fashionably, or prettier than you are? How about sizing up other coupled women and wondering why they have men and you don't? Do you get a sick feeling in your stomach when a friend calls to tell you that she has finally met the man of her dreams? Instead of feeling happy for her, you get depressed because love hasn't happened for you yet. When you experience these feelings, you are secretly wishing that the other person would suffer. The feelings of jealousy can destroy your spirit and your faith, ultimately blocking love from entering your life.

Watch an episode of any dating reality show, and you will see the green-eyed monster, jealousy, displaying itself in full force. The love connection shows are anything but loving. They demonstrate how women crawl and beg for one man who holds all of the roses. The bachelor decides who gets to stay in the make-believe mansion, and he makes his selection by comparing the women to one another. Images of Cinderella waiting for the handsome prince may start to surface in a woman's mind. These shows are far from reality because in the real world, there is more than one available man out there. Yet somehow, you forget about the abundance of men and may tend to feel competitive when you see other women vying for the guy you desire.

When you make comparisons like this and feel jealous, you are telling yourself that love is hard to find. You are holding the view that there isn't enough love and happiness for everyone. When you think that all of the good men are taken, you are left with feelings of fear, possessiveness, or jealousy. Holding these beliefs on a deep level lessens your confidence and destroys your faith. The green-eyed monster has taken over.

Why You Get Jealous

Feelings of jealousy are rooted in your younger years. At some point in your life, you wanted attention and did not get noticed or, worse, someone's interest was focused on another person instead of on you. Many families had two working parents, and quality family time was limited. Some children grew up in a large household and had many siblings, and personal attention from any parent was rare. In cases of children of divorce, many times a child is ignored by the biological parent when he or she remarries and has additional children, or the parent completely abandons the children of the first marriage to create a new family. Any of these circumstances can prompt you to create the belief that there is not enough love for everyone.

When women are jealous, they believe that there is a limited supply of men to go around. Sure, there may be a slightly higher ratio of women to men, but those statistics don't matter as much as how your inner mind is aligned with love. There could be only one single man out of a hundred men in a room, but you will be drawn to the one who is available if your mind is focused in the right place. Don't worry about anyone else. Stay aware of your wonderful unique qualities.

The Ranking System

You cannot rate yourself above certain people without believing that you rate below others. Who made up this ranking system, anyway? Was it the men, your friends, or the media? Who is the judge who determines whether you are pretty, intelligent, funny, or desirable? Is there one giant official bachelor who assigns the criteria for the perfect woman? If there was only one ideal lady, everyone who didn't fit that description would remain forever single. This is not the case because, as you may have noticed, coupled women come in all shapes, ages, colors, education levels, and personalities. When you rank yourself or others on a scale, you ignore the fact that everyone, including you, has his or her own unique beauty and gifts.

The belief that there is not enough shows up when you fear that you won't measure up to other women. Some women believe that the prettiest get picked first, and others think that their bodies must be perfect in order for men to fall in love with them. This leads to women getting face-lifts and tummy tucks and taking useless diet pills simply to make the grade. External changes are only temporary because what really matters is how you feel about yourself. If you truly believe you are enough, you naturally seem more appealing and will show up at a social event knowing that the right guy will be attracted to you. Remember, you need only *one* man.

That's Mine!

Another big reason for jealousy is the belief that the man who piques your interest is special compared to any other man. This owner-ship of a person because you saw him first, have a history with him, or slept with him is a facade. Just hang around any two-year-old or three-year-old and hear him or her exclaim "Mine!" when someone takes away the child's toy. There could be dozens of toys available to the toddler, but that one toy that he or she was playing with seems to hold all of the power. When you are dating, have you noticed a similar grasping feeling? The guy you focus on seems to be the only one in the world and you cling to this man out of desperation. You have a tantrum when he leaves.

When I was in my early twenties, I had a beach house down at the Jersey Shore. There were seven girls in our tiny three-bed-room house, which was often vacant in the evenings when the girls were off hooking up with the boys of summer. One night I was at home sleeping, and I woke up when I heard a loud crash. Then a young woman screamed, "That's my man! That's my man!" She was clawing and scratching and beating one of my roommates when she found her in bed with a guy who I assumed was "her man." I understood the anger that the young woman must have felt, seeing her boyfriend in the arms of another woman. Yet it was interesting to me that she was beating on my friend but not on "her man," who had done the cheating.

How many times have you been furious at the other woman when "your man" has gone astray? By the same token, why do women go after men who are already involved? The idea that you believe a man is yours and that he is the only man who will satisfy you is a lie that your subconscious mind tells you to keep you from seeking true love.

Being obsessed with one person can lead to destructive emotions. A divorced woman can still pine for her ex-husband, even though he cheated on her and has moved on to marry his mistress. The scorned woman gets angry at the mistress, yet still has loving feelings toward the man who broke her heart. The dark feelings that arise inside her when she hears the other woman's name can be poisonous to the mind and the body. If you are still infatuated with an ex-lover, you must first consciously decide to let him go. Focus on the negative impact your ex has had on your life and be honest with yourself. Is he really your dream man? What do you love about him?

Focusing your options for love on one person when he does not return the favor lowers your self-confidence and renders you powerless. You don't want to be the girl who is waiting to see whether the guy gives you the rose. You want to grow your own roses and find someone who has the right vase to hold the buds for you. With the power of your mind, you can transform your doubt and sense of lack into a certainty that men are bountiful and are just waiting for you to give them the nod.

Stamp of Approval

When I was single, I was guilty of being jealous of others who were happily married. I felt as if I was nothing without a man and I needed a partner to get a stamp of approval from the world. I continued to work on myself feverishly, trying to fix myself so that I could earn the right to enter the "couples club." I felt so left out when my married friends wouldn't invite me to their dinner parties because I was single. I had a sinking feeling in my stomach whenever I thought about my happy couple friends laughing, drinking wine, and having dinner while I sat home alone, sulking, with my pay-per-view movie. I wondered what was so wrong with me. What else did I need to do so that I could be a part of their blissful world? I was jealous that I didn't have access to their secret to catching a man.

After clearing my inner mind of these self-loathing beliefs, I realized that having a boyfriend wouldn't make me a better person and that not having one didn't make me any less valuable. When I took off my blinders, I could see that many of my married friends experienced the same insecurities that I did. I had the illusion that I had to be "fixed" in order for someone to love me. There is no man who can love you enough to make you love yourself. Romances never give you a one-way ticket out of self-hate, only a temporary vacation. You have to pull yourself up out of suffering.

Needing external validation is the root of jealousy. Whether you need approval from a man, society, or your family, you may seek a relationship because having a man feels like a badge of honor. You are the only one who holds the key to your personal worth. The voice in your head has more power than a million voices in the world. The chatter that you live with each day is directly responsible for the level of self-satisfaction you feel. Once you tell yourself that you are fine just the way you are, you receive your own stamp of approval.

Letting Go of Jealousy

Now that you know that jealousy isn't good for you (a shocker, right?), let's work together to find a solution to tame the green-eyed monster, once and for all. First, you have to let go of the idea that there are not enough men out there. Then let go of the belief that there is one special man who can fix what you perceive to be broken in your life. As I said before, you only need one great guy.

You are unique in your own special way. A man is out there searching for someone exactly like you. Can you imagine that? He is already somewhere in this world, waiting for you. Many men would love to be with you, and the man you are going to be with forever is on his way.

Be happy for other women when they find true love because this allows your subconscious mind to believe that love is also possible for you. You can build your confidence by loving yourself and build your own unique path to love by trusting that your time is coming, too. Changing these thoughts through self-hypnosis can easily transform your ideas of fear and scarcity to a belief in abundance and the availability of love everywhere. Your subconscious mind does not know the difference between you and other people. So if you have loving thoughts toward your married friends, your deep mind will think that being in a committed relationship is good and will drive you to that experience.

Second, understand that no one is judging you for being single. Actually, many of my married friends ultimately confessed that they were jealous of my life. Being in a relationship is not the end of all of your problems; you will simply experience different issues. There are many benefits to being single that you may forget until you meet your match, and then it is too late to appreciate them. You will always be the same person, with or without a man. The man is like a set of nice curtains. The house looks a little fancier, but it is still the same house.

Finally, learn to refocus your mind on being grateful for what you have in your life, instead of dwelling on the missing man. As I've said many times earlier, your mind creates what you concentrate on. If you give attention to being lonely and miserable, you will experience more upset feelings. By shifting your thinking to all of your wonderful blessings in life, you raise your personal vibration and attract more good things to you.

Following is a simple Gratitude exercise that you can record and play back to yourself while you are getting ready in the morning, driving to work, or preparing to go to sleep at night. You don't need to be in a hypnotic trance to experience the power of gratitude. Be sure to really feel the emotions associated with each item to get the fullest effect. A daily practice of gratitude will strengthen your attraction magnet and help you in every area to clear your subconscious mind of blockages to love.

Gratitude

Be sure to read through the entire exercise before you start.

You can either close your eyes or keep them open if you are driving or doing something else that needs your visual attention. When you begin with the first idea, imagine a small bright light inside your heart, and as each idea of gratitude is mentioned, allow the light to get brighter and brighter and ultimately expand around you as far as you like. When I mention each subject, you can pause and take as much time as necessary to gather all of the reasons that you need to be grateful and expand that light energy.

Take a deep breath and relax. First, I want you to think about the people and the animals in your life that you are most grateful for: family members, pets, friends, classmates, coworkers, neighbors, people in your life whom you don't know but see often (such as people you commute with, see at the grocery store, or pass on the street), and anyone else whom you are grateful for.

Now think of the things in your life that you are grateful for, such as your home. Go through each room and find things that you love about each one. Now move on to your car; thank it for working today. Then move on to your sports equipment: bikes, skis, golf clubs, and so on.

Then, think of the events in your life that you are grateful for: vacations, special moments with people you love, celebrations, holidays, and so on.

Next, think of your body. What do you love about your body? Be grateful for the breath that keeps you alive, the mind that helps you navigate the world and make decisions, your legs for allowing you to walk, your heart for the life force it creates in your body, and so on.

Now think of you. What do you love about *you*? Your personality, your smile, your accomplishments, your dreams—think of all the things that you love about being you.

Finally, think of the world. What do you love about the world? The sky, the water, the plants and flowers, the diversity of people, the kindness of humanity—think of all the things in the world that you are grateful for.

You are now experiencing an increased feeling of gratitude. Anytime you want to return to this feeling, say or think the word "gratitude" and all of these good feelings will come back. The word "gratitude" is a signal to your subconscious mind to bring up these wonderful emotions anytime you need them.

If your eyes were closed, count up to five and open them.

Suggestions

Feel free to say these to yourself before you count up to five, if you'd like.

I am happy when good things happen to others because I know this means good things are possible for me.

I have so many wonderful gifts in my life.

Each day, I find time to notice all of the people and things I am grateful for.

I know that constant gratitude helps attract more love into my life.

There is enough love for everyone.

I trust that I am attracting love right now.

My own self-acceptance is the only approval I need.

I am complete whether I am single or part of a couple.

I embrace my single status because I know my experience is only temporary.

I see everyone around me as being equally deserving of love.

Reinforcing Your Experience

I hope you enjoyed the feeling of gratitude and can feel the change inside. This is probably the easiest and most powerful exercise in the book. Find time to practice gratitude every day, and your life will change dramatically. If you like, you can use your affirmation bracelet to think of one item per bead that you are grateful for in your life. Or, find a unique piece of jewelry that you can wear every day to remind yourself to be grateful. Don't underestimate how the power of increasing your gratitude vibration enables you to attract the love of your life. One good thought follows another.

12

Feeling Desperate When Dateless

*At the innermost core of all loneliness is a deep and powerful
yearning for union with one's lost self.*

—Brendan Francis

Understanding Loneliness

Every single woman at one time or another has had the experience
of loneliness. Be open to the experience of being alone, and accept
what being alone means to you. The difference between being
lonely and being alone is that lonely is a *feeling* and alone is a
situation. Attaching a sad feeling to the state of being alone creates loneliness. You may feel lonely in the middle of a large crowd

or while in an unhappy relationship. The fact that someone else is in the room doesn't matter. The real issue is how you *feel* about where you are in each moment. Having faith that your alone time is temporary will lift your spirits and create a space for love to enter your life.

Your inner mind already has an understanding of what being alone feels like. These feelings probably had their origins in your childhood. If you try to get a man in order to avoid aloneness, this will create tension and desperation, qualities that can repel potential mates. Almost every woman has had experiences with guys who came on to them way too strong. You felt the man's neediness and simply wanted to run away. Don't you realize that men can feel your desperation, too? By discovering how to release the anxiety of loneliness, you can learn to relax and accept yourself, regardless of your social status.

Your lonely feeling probably originated early in your childhood. Humans are social creatures and need one another for physical and emotional survival. There is no worse feeling than being shut out from everyone around you. These feelings really characterize abandonment in its purest form. Some children are deserted by their fathers or mothers for a variety of reasons. Some parents are incarcerated; in other situations, the father divorces the mother and forgets about his children. Some children are given up for adoption at birth and never meet their natural parents. Deep within their minds, they already carry the feeling of abandonment.

Some children live with their parents but have no emotional contact with them. Being brought up by nannies or babysitters or even left with the television to keep them company, these children can still experience a sense of being ignored. The parents may have had good intentions and did not mean to neglect the children. If a parent works multiple jobs to make ends meet or has too many children to manage, this can limit the amount of love and nurturing that is available. Whatever your life circumstances may have been, every person recalls at least one event when he or she felt alone or left behind.

You were initially incarnated in a nice, warm liquid sack inside your mother. For most infants, this place is safe, predictable, and loving. The moment you enter the world, you leave a 98.7-degree warm environment and get propelled into a cold, dry, 70-degree room (an almost 30-degree drop in temperature). No wonder you scream! Your first initiation into the cold, unpredictable world is quite shocking to the senses. Now physically separate from your mother, you are incapable of controlling when she holds you, feeds you, or talks to you. For the rest of your life, you will search for that warm, comfortable, safe place where you know everything is okay.

This idea is reinforced by every experience in your young life. You continue this search for your safe place as you grow up and find a group of peers to feel connected with, and you ultimately search for Mr. Right to fill that gap. If you are one of those women who feels extremely lonely without a man, you are refusing to see other options to satisfy your need to connect. You may look at the world as unsafe until Prince Charming rescues you.

I remember being so lonely that I felt as if I was helplessly treading water in a huge ocean. I could not relax until a man came along to be my lifeboat, my island, my shore. Many of my clients report that their loneliness feels like a gaping hole in their bodies. The sensation can be quite scary because your subconscious mind is remembering your birth and interpreting your situation as life or death.

When you were a baby, if no one came to feed you, change you, or hold you, you would die. These instinctual emotions of survival are natural for both animals and people. Yet this fearful reaction conditions your subconscious mind from the very beginning of your existence to think that you need something external to save you. You allow your external environment to dictate your internal state of mind. Relying on outside forces renders you powerless as you tap into the fear of death. Your body reacts with a stress response, and your thoughts quickly follow suit with desperate chatter, looking for a way to fix the problem. The easiest way to transcend this experience is to face the fear of loneliness directly and change the story line about your social situation.

The Impact of Desperation on Your Dating Life

There are obvious reasons that desperation does not support attracting a healthy relationship. First, you are dwelling on your feelings of deficiency, believing that you lack love, which negatively affects your energy and your spirit. This downtrodden mental and emotional state will beckon the universe to bring more lack of love into your life. Second, any man whom you meet will ultimately be repelled if you have needy feelings in relation to him. He might not notice your insecurities at first, but your anguish will be laid bare as you push for a commitment too soon, are overly accommodating and available, act clingy, or are jealous in your communications. Some women are great actors and can keep their desperate persona hidden. The men will eventually pick up on these women's desolation, however, and suddenly lose interest without knowing exactly why. Finally, your level of confidence will dwindle because desperation makes you disregard personal boundaries simply to keep the man and, worse, leads you to put yourself into dangerous, physically or mentally abusive situations to avoid being alone.

When you feel lonely, you are telling yourself a sad story with a future tragic ending. You fill your mind with images of a gray-haired spinster wearing a housecoat who lives with ten cats. You exaggerate that you will never be loved, will never have children, and will die old and alone. You start to believe that someone has to save you from this awful demise. Searching for a man to come to your rescue, you forget that you have the power to change the story. If you free yourself from depending on a man to satisfy your needs, you will gain control of the narrative in your head, and this will ultimately make you a more attractive catch.

My good friend Lana is someone who has mastered being alone. She hardly ever feels lonely. Unlike most women during the breakup of a relationship, she felt excited about being alone after she separated from her ex-fiancé. She really knew how to nurture herself, and she loved the space in her single life. The last thing she wanted was to find another man. Being independent was more natural for her than for other women I have known. The only difference between my friend and other friends who felt lonely was in how Lana interpreted her situation. She saw herself as being in her full power when she was alone, in control of her schedule and environment. When she was ready to date again, she did not miss a beat. She quickly attracted a great guy because she was so relaxed and confident about her life.

Releasing the Tension of Being Alone

As I mentioned earlier, the lonely feelings are not related to your social status as much as they are to the initial event that caused the trauma and started the story line. In order to clear away your lonely feelings, you will first work with a hypnosis exercise and then move on to learn tips on how to refocus your mind through action and faith. If you don't experience any lonesome feelings, you can skip the following exercise and go directly to the tips at the end of the chapter.

SELF-HYPNOSIS

Being Alone

Be sure to read through the entire exercise before you start.

Find a comfortable place to relax, and use your favorite hypnotic-induction technique. Suggestions for inductions: do a progressive relaxation, or imagine watching the clouds float by and count backward from ten to one.

Imagine yourself in a beautiful place surrounded by nature. Take in all of the sights, smells, and sounds and begin to feel connected with the beauty around you.

There's a part of you that feels lonely and desperate. I want you to connect with that part of yourself. Inside, try to feel that void or unmet need. Now picture that need as a younger you with her hands held out, waiting for a hug. Notice how old she is. If you feel comfortable, take her into your arms and hold her.

Know that you can give her anything she wants. Ask her what she really wants. She may respond by saying love, safety, calmness, peace, and so on, and whatever she says, think of a time in your life when you felt that way or think of someone who made you feel that way (grandmothers are always good people to think about for this feeling). Imagine that feeling being a beautiful color glowing all around you, enfolding you and loving you.

Find that "void" inside yourself and fill up the space with this good feeling. Imagine this loving feeling connecting with all of the natural elements around you, the earth, the sky, the plants, the animals, the trees, and so on. Feel a beautiful beam of light coming down from the sky, and allow your spiritual source, God, the Greater Self, Love, the Universe, or whatever name you use for this divine energy to come down and surround you. Feel a beautiful being, a guardian angel, your higher self, or a spirit guide appear next to you and offer you loving assistance, letting you know that you are never alone.

Think of a word that anchors this connected feeling and say the word three times, either aloud or in your mind. Anytime you want to feel this feeling, simply say or think that word, and the feelings of connectedness will return.

Count up to five and open your eyes.

Suggestions

Feel free to say these to yourself before you count up to five, if you'd like.

I am whole and complete.

I am surrounded by love at all times.

I embrace my single status and appreciate all of the benefits I get from being single.

I always have people around me who keep me company.

I have healthy relationships in my life.

There are plenty of people who love and adore me.

I find ways every day to feel good about myself.

I enjoy my alone time.

I love discovering my wonderful self.

I give myself love and support whenever I need it.

Acceptance of Your Single Status

You may wonder why it is beneficial to accept your single status when you want to be in a relationship. Acceptance does not mean that you are resigned to being single, only that you have let go of the tension around your situation. You can look at being single as a temporary life situation, not as your life!

In this instant, you cannot change your life circumstance, so you can either resist your experience or accept it as your love life evolves. What you resist persists. If you oppose your single status, your thoughts will be occupied exclusively by what you don't want, which keeps you stuck in your single predicament.

The circumstances in your life are neutral; you are the one who decided to be unhappy. Think of this scenario: What if you knew for a fact that you would meet your guy one year from now? One year! Yes, I know it seems so far off, but what if this prophecy was *guaranteed*? How would you act? Would you relax, knowing that he was definitely showing up, and find other ways to occupy your time instead of obsessing about your dating life?

If you embrace your single status knowing that your situation is temporary and can change at any moment, this is a powerful way to let go of desperation. Something amazing happens deep in your mind as you become more loose and flexible and learn to welcome changes. You begin to accept yourself, the world around you, and your life. Having unwavering faith and expecting the best, regardless of your current circumstances, will fuel your thoughts and actions in the direction of love.

Just because you relax a bit does not mean that you stop taking action. You never know when the man of your dreams will enter your world. Use your action plan to expand your social circles and find other ways to occupy your time. You will be surprised to discover that when you are single, finding joy can be easy. You may just end up like my friend Lana and start to love your independence.

Reinforcing Your Experience

Use daily self-hypnosis to continue reinforcing your new, supportive core beliefs to stay on track. Find ways to fill up your calendar with fun events so that you don't sit at home sulking. Write a list of everything that's great about being single. You may find this exercise difficult at first, but you will probably be surprised at what you uncover.

13

Letting Down Your Guard and Opening Your Heart

Nothing external to you has any power over you.

—Ralph Waldo Emerson

Most of my clients get to a point where they feel stuck and are frustrated because "the one" has not yet appeared in their lives. They are doing all of the right things—having faith, listening to self-hypnosis programs—but these women still haven't attracted that one special person because a simple unconscious block has not yet been addressed. If this is you, there is probably a part of you that is not completely emotionally available for love. You may need to dissolve any remaining walls around your heart that are still holding you back. These walls represent a fear of true intimacy and must be addressed before you are able to let love in. Fear of intimacy is more than merely being afraid of physical contact and sex; you are avoiding a much deeper, more honest connection with another human being.

Stepping Out of Your Comfort Zone

Do you find that when a nice guy comes along, you reject him for having some ridiculous flaw, while an unavailable guy seems so much more appealing? Or, do you never go out on dates because there is no one whom you find remotely appealing enough to even share a cup of coffee with? If you consistently discard good guys, you should look within yourself to figure out what part of *you* is not available for love. To have a healthy relationship, you must be willing to step outside of your comfort zone and be open to emotional intimacy with your new partner. Some women can take off their clothes easily but find it more difficult to be emotionally naked with someone.

Many single women feel uncomfortable when men act really interested in them. You may think that there must be something wrong with a guy if he showers so much attention on you (especially if you aren't used to being treated well). Feeling turned off because a man is interested in you should be a warning that your mind is not in alignment for love. You will not allow another person to like you if you don't like yourself. If you see a pattern of always running away from the nice guys, there could be a deeper issue here: being afraid of love.

Why would anyone be frightened of love? If you don't feel as if you are worthy of being adored, you will keep everyone at arm's length. You will lock a man out of your inner world because you don't want him to discover your darkest parts. Drawn to unavailable men, you may find that superficial ties feel much safer.

The walls that remain inside you, separating you from your true love, were originally created to protect you. You learned to hold back. Often, little girls have fathers who are distant and unapproachable.

They never had the experience of being nurtured by a man. Or, you may have reached out to your father or another male figure in your life with your arms wide open, only to be rejected or turned away. The pain of that event was so intense that you vowed never to open your heart again.

Women who have been sexually abused by a family member or raped at any time in their lives created emotional barriers to protect themselves during the moments of violation. When later approached by true, caring men, these women forget about the blocks that are deep inside of them, yet they still act under the influence of these blocks. They discount the love coming toward them and push the men away as if something is wrong with these men. Being cautious is one thing, but being completely unavailable emotionally is another.

Kristie, a thirty-five-year-old court administrator, had been a victim of rape when she was twelve years old. When she began to date, if a guy came on too strong, she quickly cut him off. His advances might have been honorable and not even sexual, but she kicked him out of her life without giving him a chance. Instead, she was drawn to men who never called, were unavailable, and often lived far away. After years of therapy, she thought she was over the wounds of her rape and had a good level of self-confidence. Yet she wondered why she still wasn't satisfied with anyone she dated. By cutting out the nice guys, she was actually keeping the part of herself that wanted love hidden away. On the surface, she wanted a man to rescue the wounded twelve-year-old, but she unconsciously kept every eligible, upstanding suitor away. In order to allow a man to get close, she would have to heal the little girl first.

When she realized that she was the one who needed to love that little girl and set her free, she began the process of opening her heart. Her subconscious believed that men could not be trusted and that nice guys must be faking. To turn her love life around, she faced the child and released the trauma on a deep level so that she could be open to receiving love. Once her subconscious mind had been transformed in its ideas about men and she took charge of protecting her vulnerable side in a positive way, she started to give the nice guys a shot. As the wounded part healed, she became strong enough to feel safe around a man, knowing that she was in control regardless of his actions.

The Power of Self-Expression

Through the freedom of self-expression, you allow yourself to shine and open up to new possibilities in your relationships. The lasting benefit is that you can experience an enduring, harmonious partnership when you find your mate because you are truly being yourself, without feeling a constant need for approval. When you stop hiding behind your wounds for fear of rejection, you can step out into the world with strength and be in control of your own self-worth.

I also experienced the wall inside myself when I was faced with the prospect of true intimacy. I was afraid that if I showed my feelings, something terrible would happen. People would turn away from me in horror or, worse, laugh at me. I never had enough confidence to express what I wanted or needed. If a guy did not call when he said he would, I would plan ahead what I would say when he did call and explain how he had hurt me. When the opportunity presented itself, however, my throat tightened in resistance and I pretended that nothing was wrong. I thought I was keeping the peace and not making waves. What I didn't realize at the time was that my inability to stand up for myself was a turnoff to most men. I was considered a pushover.

In my desperate need for approval, I put my own needs aside and did everything to appease the man, which included never speaking up. This issue came into full view when I attended a seminar just before I met my husband, Roberto. The funny thing was, I hadn't taken the class for myself but instead wanted to learn some additional tools to use with my clients. This weekend turned out to be one of the most transforming events of my life.

During the event, the teachers put pressure on us to call the people in our lives with whom we had any unfinished business and to express anything that had been left unsaid. This included making apologies, setting boundaries, and conveying our love for these people. As I listened to the speaker, I thought there was no possible way that I could call my dad. My father would think I was nuts. Just the thought of talking to my dad on such a personal level made me very uncomfortable. I continued to stew about how I could get out of calling my dad when I pieced together a larger issue I'd never addressed.

I was afraid to face not only my dad with my true feelings but every man I had dated in the past as well. My mind raced back to each relationship and how it had ended without a direct confrontation. I had either laughed off the rejection or avoided the phone call. I had been running away from men and honest communication my entire life!

My mind then jumped to the letter I wrote to my dad after I attended hypnotherapy school. I told him how much I appreciated him, and my mother said that he had been very touched. Yet I never mentioned the letter when I spoke to him on the phone that week. My father had to bring up the note in our conversation. I quickly brushed him off by saying, "Yes, I meant all of that. I do love you." My efforts to communicate remained on the surface, as if there was a glass wall between me and my father. So many things were still left unsaid.

This was especially surprising to me because I felt like I was a really open and honest person. I never hide my feelings with my friends. I let myself be vulnerable with healers, classmates, and even coworkers whom I barely know. Why did I have such a difficult time being authentic around men? Even after all of this knowledge, I still was not convinced that I should call my dad. I tried to rationalize that calling him wouldn't do any good or wouldn't change anything. So I avoided making the call during the seminar break.

As the day progressed, I felt as if the teacher was talking directly to me, especially when he asked the audience who had made their phone calls. I wanted to shrink and disappear. He then said something that forever changed my life, "If you do not complete this situation with your parents, you will never have a healthy relationship." Ouch. There it was. This was the perfect opportunity to break free of this issue. Why was I even hesitating?

I'd held back from expressing myself because I was desperately seeking other people's approval. Not believing that my opinions were valid, I shoved my true feelings aside and said what I assumed the other person wanted to hear. I realized that this behavior had not given me the results I wanted, so I needed to make a change. I was terrified that I could not handle another rejection from my dad. If he brushed me off, it might crush me.

With trembling hands, I picked up the phone and dialed my dad's number. My voice quivered as I left a desperate message on his answering machine. "Dad, um, ah, I need to talk to you. I will call you back later. Don't worry, I'm all right." I hung up, disappointed with myself. Why did I fall apart like that? I was full of fear and uncertainty. Yet somehow I knew I was on the right track, even though I felt so terrible.

At the next break, I retrieved a voice mail from my mom asking me what was wrong. My parents were very concerned that I was hurt or in trouble. I quickly called my dad back. We had an amazing conversation. I told him that I didn't feel close to him and that it was my fault. I was the one holding back from really opening up to him because I was afraid. He reminded me that he had not been brought up to be communicative and affectionate. I told him that I wanted to make an effort to be more open and close to him. I didn't want us to go through our entire lives feeling separate and disconnected. He agreed that he also wanted a better relationship with me. We talked for about ten minutes more. Believe it or not, this was the longest and deepest conversation that we'd ever had.

I hung up the phone and felt a heaviness instantly lift off me. I was completely blown away at how my dad had responded to me. I thought he would give his typical yes and no answers or, worse, laugh off my attempt at communication as a joke. Our conversation had been better than I ever could have imagined. I felt as if the little girl inside me had been waiting her entire life for a hug from her daddy, and she finally got it. Even if he'd responded differently, I would have been able to handle it. The important thing is that I finally made the effort. When I spoke from the heart, amazing things happened.

After that weekend, I felt different. My desperation to find a man to love me was dissolving away. I knew that I would be so much more powerful in my relationships now, with the freedom to express myself while knowing I had nothing to lose. All of those false beliefs that the little girl inside me had held about men not loving her were now baseless. I *was* lovable.

Learning to Avoid Manipulative Communication

What is holding you back from really experiencing your authentic power? Do you try to phrase your words in order to get a certain response? The reason my communication with my dad was so life-changing was because the conversation was real. I didn't plan my words so that he would respond in a certain way. Honoring my own self-expression was the only result I was attached to, regardless of his response. When you communicate honestly while not fearing the other person's reaction, you become empowered.

Many women discuss with one another how to approach a man about an issue. They debate with their girlfriends for hours as to the best way to phrase their concerns to make sure that the man doesn't leave and she gets what she wants. This is a sales tactic that results in attracting a man who reacts to your superficial self. Is that who you really want?

Sure, you can use many communication styles to be more effective in what you say, but you shouldn't use them to garner a specific reaction. Perhaps you throw your words like a boomerang, while expecting a predictable response in return. You may be afraid of the man's telling you that he doesn't like you or doesn't want to be with you. But why would you even want to influence a person like this to stay in your life? Tying yourself to the man's reaction leaves you powerless and, ultimately, unattractive.

What would you be like if you simply said what you felt without trying to manipulate a specific response out of the other person? Imagine stating your needs and letting go of the outcome. This freedom does belong to you. Your mind argues that if you show your hand, you will be in trouble. Words spoken are hard to take back, so be clear on what you want to say before you blurt out your ideas. If your guy is meant to be with you, he won't leave because you expressed yourself authentically. He may even be convinced to stay.

Claire, a twenty-five-year-old student, came to me because she had been dating Paul for a few months and wasn't sure where their relationship was going. She rarely spoke up for herself with men and always went with the flow, allowing the courtship to take its own course without putting pressure on the guy to commit. Each relationship she'd had lasted about three months and then slowly burned out. Fearing that Paul would break up with her, she never questioned his level of commitment, even when he started to leave her home alone on weekends while he went skiing with his buddies.

I asked her what she really wanted, and she said, "A committed relationship that leads to marriage and children." I questioned Paul's behavior and whether he fit into what she truly wanted. She really liked Paul and felt a strong physical connection when they were together. She rationalized that their relationship was too new for her to place any demands on him. I then asked her whether she knew what he wanted, and she hesitated with a puzzled look. "No, I never even thought to ask," she said, realizing that they'd never discussed their expectations with each other. The only way she'd get the relationship she wanted was to speak up.

The next time Paul told her that he was going skiing for the weekend, Claire interjected and expressed her feelings about being left alone on weekends. She clarified to him that this was not the kind of relationship she was seeking. At first, Paul backpedaled and gave excuses, but then he quickly shifted his position because he was afraid to lose Claire. He told her that he didn't want to lose her and would be willing to change. Paul's respect and honor for her increased in exact proportion to her own self-respect. Claire and Paul got engaged about a year later, and they always ski together on weekends.

This story has a happy ending, but not all confrontations lead to a blissful reconnection. If Paul had decided to end things, Claire might have been hurt at first, but she would have avoided wasting her energy on a dead-end relationship. By stating her needs, she increased her confidence and sent a signal to her subconscious that she was worthy of more. Many times my clients have asked their boyfriends for a stronger commitment, and the men left them. In these cases, the old relationship had to move out so that true love could enter these women's lives.

You can never predict how someone will respond to your words. No matter how much you finely craft your dialogue, the other person is always free to respond any way he or she may like. People can also sense when you are trying to manipulate them, so your efforts to influence them may be futile. If you say what you want, you usually end up getting what you ask for. Be open to receiving, in whatever form your wish arrives. Someone may step into your life to answer your call. You release the walls inside yourself when you stop feeling so vulnerable and powerless in communication.

Diving into the Shallow End

Instead of running away from the nice guys, what if you are someone who is addicted to the overwhelming attention of a lover's pursuit? Instant romances can be a temporary salve for a lonely heart, but as the high of infatuation fades, you move on to the next victim. These quickie flings can also keep you from experiencing real intimacy because they are based on superficial communication. You may believe you are in love because the illusion is so strong, but the lack of substance cannot hold the relationship together for the long haul.

I recently read a post on a dating site written by a woman who was critical of her friend's attraction to a new love interest because he bought her a birthday present two days after they met. The so-called expert immediately judged the man to be insecure and needy and said that her friend was also desperate. The advice columnist predicted that the relationship would be a crash-and-burn, doomed for disaster.

I understand why she said this. Many extremely intense relationships come into being because of a surface need for a partnership. One or both parties want a mate so much that they create a fantasy romance with someone they barely know. They may become infatuated because of their physical attraction, a hope for financial security, or the romantic environment where they met. For example, when two people meet at a wedding, during the holidays, or on vacation, this can create an illusory aura around the relationship. Just like in those reality shows, which are far from reality, the externally attractive singles create a facade of romance in staged exotic dates and movielike moonlight dinners. Or if you are old enough you may remember *The Love Boat* and how intense every relationship became when the two people had only seven days with each other. Maybe Rose and Jack really did love each other, but would their connection have been different if they'd met somewhere else besides the ill-fated *Titanic*? That ship sunk, just as many of these fly-by-night affairs do.

The reason people can quickly fall for each other and then easily run away is that their feelings are very superficial. Each party idolizes the other, putting the other person on a pedestal. Then the relationship immediately shifts into the "instant couple syndrome." They spend every night together, and eventually they start to see each other in the light of day. Even though they are both good people, they are destined to fall off the high pedestals they created for each other.

If you dismiss these instant romances as fake, however, think again. They can be powerful forces of change in your life. Every person is attracted to you based on your level of self-acceptance.

If two people are feeling insecure and they meet, they could easily fall into an intense relationship that does not necessarily have
to end in tragedy. Imagine that these two lost souls awaken from
the dream and into the reality of their true selves. Through their
union, they increase each other's confidence and belief in their ability to be loved. Instead of awakening and running away, they could
embrace each other's foibles and learn to love on a deeper level
than before.

These instant romances are not always created by insecurity,
either. Depending on your clarity of mind and what you want, a new
romance may be intense and may also last many years. If you are
open to your own intuition, you may truly find your perfect match
and might know it immediately. Only you are the judge as to how
much you know yourself and whether this is an old pattern or something new. If you are meant for each other, why wait and conduct
yourself according to predetermined dating rules that merely postpone your inevitable destiny together?

I worked with a client named Shannon who was forty-two
and had never been married. She was a very beautiful woman
and always had men in her life. She had recently broken up with
her latest short-term boyfriend when she came to me looking for
answers as to why she could not have a healthy relationship. Her
pattern was to quickly fall for a guy on the first date, get into an
immediate deep relationship, and then end the relationship within
two months.

She really wanted to have a boyfriend and became infatuated
with every new man who seemed to fit her requirements. Jumping
into romance head first, she and the man would sleep together right
away, declare their love too soon, and take the express lane toward a
committed relationship. When I told her that she was blocking love,
she was surprised because she always felt so open and ready for a
partnership.

I told Shannon that the reason she got bored was that she was
in love with the idea of being in love, instead of with the man who

was in her life. She was addicted to the high of the passion, which was really a shallow connection between her and a stranger. The fantasy in her mind was much better than the reality. By moving on to the next person, she never had to worry about being truly open and intimate on a deeper level.

Many men operate on this premise as well. A mama's boy usually has an unrealistic expectation of the woman of his dreams and will dump a woman who starts to become human. On the other hand, if a parent abandoned the boy, he may grow up to have one superficial fling after another and ultimately leave the women in his life. These so-called womanizers are not confident but are really fearful of rejection. They get their power from being in control of the abandonment.

If you fall into relationships blindly, too quickly, and too often, you may be desperately attempting to grasp on to anyone who comes along, hoping that he will save you. Again, you seek salvation from the external, because you feel like nobody until someone defines you as lovable. You reach out for love as if for scraps of food in a soup kitchen, taking whatever they bring you. Like a skimming stone bouncing across the top of the water, you never stay long enough to really get to know the other person, and you jump out of the relationship as quickly as you entered it. The only way to experience love is to take a chance by diving into the deep end and not being afraid to go under water every once in a while. You will always float to the surface again.

Opening Your Heart and Being Available for Love

Whether you hide out, avoid speaking your mind, or skim from one surface romance to another, the result is always the same. You keep real love out. By increasing your faith, you can start to believe that you will be taken care of and protected in any circumstance. The following exercise will open your heart and prepare you for a healthy love relationship. Even after you clear out some of your old baggage from the past, the fear of getting too close may be standing between you and Mr. Right. The only cure is unwavering faith in yourself and your amazing power.

SELF-HYPNOSIS

Let Love In

Be sure to read through the entire exercise before you start.

Find a quiet place and get comfortable. Close your eyes and take a few deep breaths. Allow a peaceful relaxing energy to move from the top of your head all the way down to your toes. Feel your breath move through your body as if it is coming out of every pore in your skin, while you breathe in and out. Scan your body, starting at your head, and move down to find any parts of your body that are holding tension. Imagine that you can squeeze the tension a bit more and then relax it when you exhale. Breathe deeper. Feel the relaxing energy move all through your body as if your hands and feet are also breathing out all tightness and letting go.

Picture yourself in a simple white room with four walls and a window that looks out onto a beautiful nature scene. You can decorate the room any way you like. Add furniture, pictures, tables, plants, and so on—anything you need to feel comfortable in your own special room. Make sure that you place objects in the room that help you feel safe and secure.

After you are finished decorating, imagine yourself relaxing in a comfortable chair. Cover your body with a thick, warm blanket. You may visualize having some candles lit and a book to read; perhaps you have a glass of wine or a cup of tea. Everything you imagine makes you feel even more comfortable, more relaxed.

You can be safe and peaceful here in the room of your life. You sometimes get lonely, but it seems like it is simply too much effort to get up from your comfortable place to make any changes in your life.

Then . . . there is a knock at the door. Instinctively, you know that a man is standing outside with a beautiful bouquet of flowers. He's a stranger, but somehow he knows that you are the right person for him. He wants to be with you. He has honorable intentions. You know that he poses no threat to your safety, but somehow you think it's too much trouble to get up and answer the door. So you do nothing. You sit there and hide.

There is a conflict inside you because part of you wants to jump up and open the door, but a stronger part of you has intense resistance. Get in touch with the resistant part of yourself now. Think of it as a heavy armor of protection, so heavy that it keeps you from getting up and answering the door. There is a word written on this armor that surrounds you in false protection. Try to read what that word is. Determine what this armor represents to you. You may also see an age etched in the armor that indicates the year when this armor started to become a part of you. As you identify this armor, ask it for permission to be released. If the answer is yes, visualize the armor lifting up and away from you and dissolving into the ceiling. If you like, you can ask your angels or guides to help you release it.

After the armor is released, think of your "good feeling" and color and surround yourself with the "good feeling" again. This feeling is a protective energy that allows only partners with higher vibrations into your life, but at the same time it is an energy that lets you open up to receive love. You can also visualize your heart space opening like a beautiful flower until you feel the love waiting for you.

Work with the energy until you feel comfortable getting up and walking to the door. You get to choose whether you want to open the door and talk to your future love in the doorway or whether you would like to invite him into your safe place.

Once you connect with your future love, you can ask him questions and see whether there are any remaining blocks inside you that would prevent you from attracting him into your life.

You can either anchor in that feeling with your "good feeling" word by saying the word three times, or you can create a new word anchor specifically for this issue.

Then, when you are ready, say good-bye to your future love for now, knowing that you can always come back to see him in your special safe place anytime you like.

Count up to five and open your eyes.

Suggestions

Feel free to say these to yourself before you count up to five, if you'd like.

It is safe for me to express myself.

I always find the right words to get my point across to other people.

I speak with authority and clearly state what I want and need.

> I release and clear all blocks to opening my heart to love.
>
> I know that it is safe to be loved.
>
> I follow my intuition and always put myself in beneficial situations.
>
> I love to show my true self to others.
>
> I can express myself with power.
>
> No matter what the response is from others, I feel good about myself.
>
> I allow the right people to get close to me.

Some people find that it takes more than one attempt at this exercise to convince their armor to be released. If you feel as if there is strong resistance, you may wish to ask whether this blockage needs any additional resources before you can release it. Be patient; sometimes the fear is stronger than we realize. Give yourself time and space to do the work. The armor will release itself when you are ready.

Remember that you are always in control of how you move through the processes in this book. Pay attention to your inner wisdom, which will guide you every step of the way. Usually, this is the last issue that my clients address before their true loves enter their lives.

Reinforcing Your Experience

Continue to condition your mind with daily self-hypnosis. Practice becoming more open with your communication and sharing your true feelings with others. Give a kind word to a stranger or tell one of your parents or someone close to you how much you appreciate him or her. Do these exercises at a pace that feels right to you.

14

Gaining Access to Your Spiritual Resources

The intuitive mind is a sacred gift and the rational mind is a faithful servant. We have created a society that honors the servant and has forgotten the gift.

—Albert Einstein

Regardless of your religious upbringing, there is a single thread of truth woven through all spiritual traditions. Guidelines such as be kind to others, do not steal or kill, and so on are the backbone of civilization. Your spiritual beliefs can carry you through your darkest times and inspire you to have faith in the unseen. You can tap into this resource using your current tradition, or expand and discover a new connection to the divine. The most important factor is to use the methods and the philosophy that resonate best with you. Faith builds an expectation that you are attracting your love any day now. You can rely on your spiritual resources to keep your mind on track in realising your highest desires.

Using Your Current Spiritual Tradition

The next time you visit your place of worship or pick up a holy text, pay attention to messages about the power of your thoughts. Concepts that I have explained in this book are based on information that has circulated throughout our civilization for thousands of years. There is nothing new here. Whatever words or parables the various traditions use will strike a chord with the universal laws of creation.

You can easily incorporate your tradition into your self-hypnosis exercises. I have worked with clients of every religion and helped them use their current spiritual viewpoint to enhance their sessions. For example, many Christians love it when in the visualization I include Jesus coming in to assist in their healing. They imagine him standing over them with his healing hands or holding them in his arms. Non-Christian clients simply imagine God's energy flooding their bodies. Even atheists have imagined bringing in the earth's energy to balance their fears and lift their burdens. If you use your faith as an added bonus in your sessions, this will improve the results. Even if you haven't practiced your faith in years, you can benefit from reconnecting to your divine source. You may also choose to expand your belief system and discover a new relationship with your divine self.

Discovering or Expanding Your Divine Connection

Maybe you were brought up within a specific religious tradition and are no longer practicing. I am not going to discuss which spiritual resource you should use, but I'll explain your options so that you can discover your own way. You can use your current belief system and take your faith to the next level. My Christian clients use Jesus as a healing image but also expand their visualizations to include angels, light beings, deceased relatives, spirit guides, and even power animals. Many of my clients use crystals, prayer beads, and other tokens to enhance their sessions. There is no right or wrong way to incorporate your spirituality into the process. Your way is personal and unique to you. Your faith is all that is required. What works for some people does not work for others. That is why there are so many different types of belief systems, healers, shamans, and therapists.

Using Spirit Guides, Angels, or Fairies

You may find comfort in knowing that beings on the other side are willing to help you find your man. Some of my clients imagine their deceased relatives (a grandparent, for example) guiding them. If you have never worked with celestial beings and want to try that, here are some ideas to get started.

Anytime, whether you are in a hypnosis session or simply walking down the street, you can mentally talk to celestial beings. Ask them to help you find your man or give you a sign. If you would like a formal communication, call them in to your hypnosis visualization. Here is a brief example of what I incorporate into my sessions with single clients who believe in angels:

You are standing in a beautiful place holding scrolls in your hand. On these scrolls you have written your list of qualifications for your true love. Imagine light beams flying in from the sky approaching you, turning into your relationship angels [spirit guides/fairies]. Hand them each a scroll with instructions to have them help you draw this man into your life. You see them turn into beautiful beams of light and fly out to the world on their mission to help you find your true love.

Some clients cannot make out the shapes of the beings and sense them only as pure light. Either way, simply believe that the spiritual helpers are there in whatever form you can perceive.

Don't worry about seeing them. Some people receive information from their angels or guides through signs. Pay attention to synchronicities that appear in your life after your request. If you receive an invitation to a party, maybe the angels were helping you out. Sometimes the sign comes in repetition. If you see a commercial frequently or hear a song repeated in the same day, the message could be from your angels or guides. The messages may come in the form of an overheard conversation, a sign on the road, or a phone call from a friend you have not heard from in years. Most people cannot have a regular dialogue with their angels or guides, so the spiritual beings communicate through other means.

Before you scoff at these methods for being irrational magical thinking or even for defying the laws of physics, keep in mind that many great minds believed in similar concepts. Carl Jung theorized that an acausal connecting principle was at work in the universe, in addition to the causal one we are most familiar with (causal meaning that event A causes event B, which causes event C). With the acausal connecting principle or, as he termed it, *synchronicity*, like attracts like. Similar thoughts, actions, and objects clump together in a nonrandom manner. He wrote about examples of synchronicity in his own life, most famously the one involving a beetle. Once while in his study he was reading about Egyptian scarabs, and he heard a tiny click that kept being repeated over and over. He looked around and traced the sound to a beetle that was inexplicably flying into the glass of his window, as if trying to get inside. Jung believed that his own focused thinking about Egyptian scarabs had drawn a living beetle to approach him.

Here are two fun exercises that I do when I want to receive an answer from the universe to one of my burning questions.

Exercise

The Radio

When you want more information about a man, a decision, or even a business deal, try the Radio exercise. Think about your issue and ask for a sign. Then turn on the radio and listen to the very first words that you hear (whether a song or talk radio). This is your answer.

I do this all the time. Once I was thinking about a guy whom I was not sure about (okay, there were hundreds of those times), and I turned on the radio and heard "You should just forget him." I was tuned in to a sports radio station and the hosts were talking about a baseball player. I couldn't believe what I had just heard. Another time, I was wondering about another one of my temporary men and wanted to know whether he was trustworthy. The song "Run-Around" by Blues Traveler came on and confirmed my suspicions about this man.

I also used this technique when someone had broken into my car and stolen my backpack filled with thousands of dollars' worth of checks and my handwritten client schedule. I was not too worried about the checks (I called my clients and had them stop payment), but my schedule was another story. I was booked for the next four weeks, but I had no client phone numbers or any other record of their appointments except in that book. I had resolved to sit in my office for a month and wait to see who showed up. I drove to the bank and prayed that my bag would return to me. I asked my angels to find my bag or at least retrieve my schedule. I then turned on the radio and the song lyric I heard was "I'll keep working my way back to you, babe." Not more than two seconds later, I received a phone call from a man who lived in the neighborhood where my car had been vandalized. He told me that he had my belongings. Everything was there: the bag, the checks, and the schedule. I love my angels!

Exercise

The Book

Similar to the Radio exercise, you can also ask your question, open a book to any page, and randomly point to a word (or a string of words) for your answer. You can use whatever book you choose to receive communication from your angels.

I am told there are many types of angels for all of life's issues. You can be specific and call in your relationship angels, your money angels, and your health angels whenever you need them. Even if you don't believe in angels, you can use the asking technique directly to the universe or to God and watch what shows up.

Getting in Touch with Your Higher Self

Another way to gain access to a spiritual resource is to look within yourself. You can tap into the energy that infuses your body and mind. Some people call this force the aura or the energy field. It can be felt when you get into deeper states of trance or during peak moments in your life. Experience the direct connection to who you are beyond your physical form and the conscious and subconscious thoughts in your mind. This pure energy can be felt as unconditional love and is sometimes referred to as the superconscious. For some people, getting in touch with this power is like directly experiencing God or the divine.

In a meditation or a visualization, you can easily feel the energy that is all around you. If you require a more tangible image of God or the divine, design your own image. Be creative and come up with something that works within your unique belief system. You can use the image of a goddess, a white-robed wise man, or something really outside the box. This private experience is yours alone, so do whatever you like. If you want to connect with your divine self or a higher power during a visualization, you can get answers on the spot. It may take practice for some people to open up and receive clear information, but you can learn to get better at receiving impressions. Here is a brief exercise to include in your visualization to help you access your divine self and receive inspiration and guidance:

Imagine sitting in a beautiful chair in a spacious garden. Think of an issue and ask for guidance to come to support you. See a beautiful golden light appearing in front of you. Allow the image of your wise self to become clearer in your vision. Thank your wise self for joining you here today in this peaceful place, and ask your question. Listen silently to the reply. You may see the response in spoken words, images, or symbols. Accept whatever information you receive and open your eyes.

Take out your journal and write down your impressions. You may experience a flow of information beyond your initial visualization after you begin to write. Always add a title to your request and date the entry so that you can refer back to this information anytime you need more insight. You may also receive additional impressions in the form of a dream or a sign after the visualization and the journaling are complete. If a higher or divine self works best for you, you can also use that idea in the Radio and Book exercises described earlier in this chapter.

Increasing Your Intuition

As your mind becomes more focused on love and clear of old past baggage, you may discover that your intuitive senses are beginning to develop. This occurs because you are moving beyond your previous patterns of being and you are now consciously creating your life. Because you are more in touch with your subconscious mind and connected to the wonderful spirit within you, a new world of synchronicities, divine intervention, and miracles is opening up to you.

Although your intuition may naturally increase as you practice daily self-hypnosis, there are also some specific ways you can improve your sixth sense. Your intuition is like a muscle that needs to be worked with in order to become strong. Here are some guidelines to help you tone up your intuition:

- Pay attention to the synchronicities that appear in your life.
- Keep a journal of your intentions and the impressions you receive in your daily self-hypnosis exercises, and record your miracles.
- Try the following activities:

    Psychic tests. Give yourself some psychic tests, such as guessing the color of the shirt your date will be wearing. Psychic tests may seem like a guessing game at first. Have fun and relax with this power so that you get good "hits."

    Psychic parties. Gather a few open-minded girlfriends together and play with your intuition. Get a blank envelope and a piece of paper for everyone in attendance. Have each woman write her name on a piece of paper, fold the paper up neatly, and place it in a blank envelope. Gather and shuffle the envelopes, then pass an envelope to each person to open. Everyone should have another blank piece of paper or a notepad to write on. When you give them the nod, have everyone close their eyes and focus on the name in their envelope. Then call for ten to fifteen minutes of silence, while everyone writes down any impressions she gets, either visual images or feelings. If anyone is stuck, you can tell her to write whatever comes to her mind, and eventually some information will come through. After everyone is finished, the group can either choose to share their experiences together or do it directly with the person in private. This is a great technique if your guests don't know one another well because the information will be purer, without past history getting in the way of people's impressions. You can do this exercise in a variety of ways. For example, have each person bring a personal item (preferably something that's not obviously identifiable), instead of writing her name on the paper. Have each person hold an object belonging to another person and write down her impressions. Or, you may want to have the entire group focus on one person. The group can compare notes for accuracy after everyone's impressions have been received.

Tarot cards or inspiration card decks. There are a plethora of tarot cards and inspiration cards on the market that you can use for daily readings. Be sure to note the individual cards you select in your journal so that you can track the results. If you are inclined, purchase a tarot deck and a book for beginners and read your own tarot cards. To keep it simple, you can pick three cards: one for the past, one for the present, and one for the future. I have done this at parties and gave readings to my friends that were astoundingly accurate.

Dreams. This is my favorite way to receive psychic input from the divine. Keep a dream journal and pay attention to recurring patterns in your dreams. Some hypnotists are skilled with dream hypnosis and can help you work with your subconscious mind to understand the meaning of your dreams. If you are one of those people who complains that you can never remember your dreams, try this technique. Before you go to sleep, set the intention that you are going to remember your dreams. Ask the divine to give you an answer through your dreams about an issue that you want resolved. You may have to do this a few nights in a row before you start to remember your dreams. You can also do self-hypnosis using suggestions that reinforce the idea that you are beginning to recall your dreams. Keep the dream journal beside your bed, and as soon as you wake up, don't open your eyes yet because the visual stimulation will tend to make you forget your dreams. Instead, take the journal into bed with you and squint your eyes open a tiny crack, only enough to ensure that your pen is contacting the paper, or else keep them closed. Then write down your dreams. Your writing will naturally be messy, but you won't lose the thread of remembering your dreams so quickly if you keep your eyes closed.

There are many ways to increase your intuition beyond the methods I've described here. If this subject interests you, check out your local bookstore for the many books that are available on tapping into your intuitive abilities, or take a workshop or a class in your area. When you are dating a new man, you may want to keep your newfound abilities private until you know that he is open to this kind of thinking. I used to refer to expressing my unique spiritual beliefs as letting my "spiritual cat out of the bag." Even some open-minded guys with the best intentions need a little warming up before they are exposed to the awesome powers of the universe. Let's just keep it our little secret for now.

Your faith in a higher, greater power within or around you can accelerate your efforts to attract the love of your life. The benefits of being in touch with your spirituality will expand far beyond your dating life. As you discover the inner reaches of your mind, you will find that the journey is endless and fascinating. Your life will continually unfold in powerful new ways.

15

Pulling It All Together

The meeting of two personalities is like the contact of two chemical substances: if there is any reaction, both are transformed.

—Carl Jung

Now that you have come so far in transforming your inner mind, here are some tips to keep you on track in regard to meeting Mr. Right. The conditioned mind will always attempt to return to the status quo until the new information is completely absorbed. You've been the "old you" for a long time; it takes a while to become familiar with your real, lovable self. Don't get discouraged when challenges test your faith; look at obstacles as feedback that can help you stay in the lane of love.

Review of the Three Principles
of Creation

As you continue your search for the love of your life, keep in mind
that the three principles of creating what you want must work
together: thoughts, action, and faith. If one or more of these elements are out of sync, you could delay your having a healthy relationship. Your core beliefs drive your thoughts and actions and bring
you the results that you experience in life. By redirecting those beliefs
into positive expectations, you forever change the direction of your
romantic future.

1. Thoughts

   - Be clear on what you want. Continue to work with fine-
     tuning the vision of your ideal mate and mentally focus-
     ing on that idea.

   - Make sure that your subconscious mind is in alignment
     with your desire for love. If necessary, repeat the exercises
     in this book until you completely release and transform
     the core beliefs that keep you blocked from having your
     dream relationship.

   - Focus on gratitude so that you can invite more good expe-
     riences into your life.

2. Action

   - Be consistent with your actions and put yourself in situa-
     tions where you can meet new people.

   - Keep your actions aligned with your goals—stop dating
     "temporary" men.

   - When you act, keep your vision in your mind. Whether
     you are searching online for potential dates or attending a
     social event, always keep your mind clear about what you
     want and let go of desperation and past expectations.

- Continue to work with your feelings and the acceptance of all emotions.

- Remember to use feelings when you perform daily tasks and the hypnosis exercises, so that your emotions are aligned with what you want.

3. Faith

- Have unwavering faith (even if the evidence has not appeared yet) that you will attract your true love.

- Believe in the oneness of all people and that we are all connected. Remember that everyone really wants you to be happy and that there is enough love in the world for all of us.

- Increase your faith by having positive expectations. What you expect to happen is directly tied to the results you experience.

A Continuous Discovery

Your subconscious mind is filled with information that does not always support you in having a peaceful life and is continually taking on additional information from the external world. There is never a point when we are finished escaping our human emotions. Life is a continuous journey. As you uncover false beliefs and heal them, you may find that different ones are revealed. Once you turn on the light in a room, you will start to see the imperfections that you did not see when the room was dark. Many of my clients get discouraged when they work on themselves and find yet another block. The good news is that you are learning to recognize the blocks as something you can manage instead of feeling powerless toward them.

Discovering more about yourself keeps life interesting. If you look at your experience as a never-ending voyage, you will venture down into the depths of your inner being and truly get to your authentic self. Instead of dreading the blocks as you do weeds in a garden, become amazed at your power to pull them out and be free of them. Facing whatever you encounter in the depths of your mind, while believing in yourself, is the most empowering way to live.

As you awaken to newfound mental obstacles that have prevented you from reaching your goals, you can create your own personalized self-hypnosis programs to address them. All of the visualizations in this book can be used for a variety of purposes, if you would rather stick to a familiar script. To keep this book down to a reasonable size, I could not possibly include a script for every specific issue that comes up in dating and relationships. If you have a unique issue, however, create your own tape recording to transform and heal that part of yourself for good.

Developing Your Own Personalized Self-Hypnosis Program

Here are five easy steps to get you started on your own self-hypnosis program.

1. *Identify the goal*. First, be clear on the goal that you would like to work toward. Here are some goals that my clients frequently express:
   - Getting over a past relationship
   - Letting go of anger
   - Increasing confidence

   Be sure that your goal is specific, attainable, and measurable. Ask yourself this question, "How will I know if the self-hypnosis is working?" For instance, if you want to increase your confidence, what evidence would you see if your confidence had grown? Would you approach more people or notice your mind-chatter changing? Answering questions like this will help you recognize the effects when they occur and help you write powerful suggestions.

2. *Uncover your beliefs.* To effectively transform thoughts in the subconscious mind that block you from attaining your goal, you must know what the root belief is that is driving those thoughts. Discover the *exact phrases* you use in your thoughts. To continue with the example of increasing confidence, you must first figure out which thoughts running through your mind *decrease* your confidence. Thoughts such as "I am boring" or "I am fat" need to be clearly identified before you can reverse them. To revive an old trick mentioned earlier in the book, take out your journal and write at the top of a new page this phrase: *When I think about being confident [or whatever your goal is], I think I am . . .* Let your thoughts flow onto the paper without judging them. Your subconscious is doing a quick dump of all of the reasons why you should not reach your goal. This process is similar to performing a virus scan on your computer. When you state an intention, your mind will automatically search for ideas that surround that belief, whether supportive or unsupportive. Isn't that amazing? You can use this technique to uncover what the subconscious mind is retaining about any topic you want, in addition to relationships. Once you find your man, you may want to attract more money into your life or achieve better health. The possibilities are endless.

3. *Transform your beliefs.* Now that you know which thoughts are blocking you, use another page of your journal and reverse all of those ideas into something you would like to believe. If you wrote "I am boring," replace that phrase with "I am interesting." If the thought "I am stupid" arose, you can reframe the idea as "I am intelligent" or "I am knowledgeable." Make sure you include all of the new phrases in your final script.

4. *Write your script.* Gather all of the positive phrases from step 3 and elaborate on them. If you wrote "I am interesting,"

come up with the reasons that you are interesting, as well as other synonyms for the word. Be sure to include your exact language because your subconscious is more able to change when it feels that the information is coming from you. You are the one who will believe what you think about the most. Keep in mind the rules for effective suggestion writing. I have listed them here again for your easy reference:

- *Make it believable*. You must believe that your goal is attainable.

- *Stay positive*. Avoid negative words (no, won't, don't, not, and so on.)

- *Use the present tense*. Don't use the phrase "I will ..." Place every suggestion in the present tense as if your idea is already happening.

- *Simplify*. Keep it simple enough that a bright nine-year-old would understand.

- *Suggest action and use feeling words to increase your motivation*. You can also include incremental steps, such as "I am excited and feel confident about setting up my profile"; "I enjoy socializing at least three evenings per month."

- *Use repetition*. Repeat key phrases at least three times and use different words to reinforce similar ideas.

- *Emotionalize the outcome*. Engage your feelings as you visualize your future.

5. *Put your session together*. Pick out your favorite induction and deepener and peaceful place. Write out your suggestions, and add a mental movie at the end as if visualizing your goal. The visualization could consist of seeing yourself being confident in a social situation or having lots of men approach you because you feel so good about yourself. Have fun with the visualization and make sure that you *engage the feeling*.

Don't get too fancy with your first sessions. For best results, follow the simple guideline of induction, deepener, suggestions, visualization, and counting up. If you feel confident in your hypnotic abilities, feel free to throw in a posthypnotic suggestion or two.

Ways to Do Self-Hypnosis

There are many ways to do self-hypnosis. I provide a sampling of them here.

Record Your Own Programs

The easiest way to do self-hypnosis is to record the session and replay the program so that you can relax and allow your recorded voice to take you through the steps. Most computers and cell phones come with a voice recorder, so you can easily record your sessions. You can also find digital recording software on the Internet or, if you plan to invest more time and effort, get a digital recorder from an electronics store.

Make sure you have your entire script written out so that you can read through the words easily. Practice a few times before you actually do a live recording. When reading the script, be sure to speak slowly and melodically, as if you were lulling a child to sleep. Speak calmly, gently, and convincingly. Pause after certain sections to give yourself time to soak in the information or to visualize your desired result. Keep the session within ten to twenty minutes in length so that you can use the program every day. With practice, you will learn the right pitch and flow for your words that work best for you.

Final editing can be done if you have audio editing software. There are some inexpensive programs online that allow you to upload your audio and cut out parts that you don't need. This is an added step that requires a learning curve to use the software. If you are not computer savvy, stick to your program just as you originally recorded it. You will be surprised at how good you sound, even with the rough recording. Some novice hypnotists still get great results because hypnotic suggestions are so powerful.

Self-Hypnosis without a Recording

If you don't want to bother with recording your voice, you can also create a short script to memorize. Make hypnosis a ritual every morning or evening, and perform your session as if it's a meditation. Daily practice will help you remember your script and will also let you adjust and fine-tune your session as the weeks pass. Don't lie in bed when you do the session on your own. Sit up during your practice to ensure that you don't fall asleep. I don't want you to miss any work because of this!

Professionally Produced Programs

Download your free "Attract the Love of Your Life" mp3 program by using the code LLB310 and entering it on the book's Web site: www.letloveinbook.com. You will also find links to more than ninety different self-hypnosis programs that I have produced for various issues.

Professional Self-Hypnosis

If you feel that you need professional-level work, you can find a hypnotherapist or a hypnotist in your area and undergo a private session. Most sessions cost $100 to $250, depending on the practitioner's experience. Remember, though, that all hypnosis is self-hypnosis. The hypnotist is simply guiding you through the process. Having a live person lead you can be a great benefit when you are really stuck. He or she can help you navigate through your mind (just as a coach would do) and help you reach your desired outcome.

Tips on Selecting a Qualified Hypnotherapist or Coach

- Find a hypnotherapist who is certified with a reputable hypnosis association. I recommend the American Council of Hypnotist Examiners (ACHE) organization because it requires the highest levels of training in the field of hypnotherapy. There is a wide range of training for hypnotists and hypnotherapists, because the field is not currently regulated and does not require a license to practice. Do your research to make sure that you are working with someone who has at least 250 hours of training.

- Another option is to hire a Certified Hypnotic-Coach. These life coaches are specifically trained in hypnosis. Trained hypnotists have an expertise in getting you into a great trance and are able to formulate the right suggestions to achieve faster results. Simple creative visualization may feel good but might not be as effective if it does not include hypnotic suggestions. These coaches are also certified by the ACHE.

- Interview a few different hypnotists or hypnotherapists to see which one you feel most comfortable with. Ninety percent of your success is directly related to how much you like your therapist or coach.

- Call a local hypnotherapy school to get a referral. The school will typically refer you to its top graduates.

- Some hypnotherapists do phone sessions, so you can look outside your local town to widen your selection. I primarily do phone sessions, and I find them more effective because the client can relax at home in his or her own environment. No touching is involved, and your eyes are closed anyway, so it does not matter where you and the hypnotist are located.

Hypnotize with a Friend

You can write out your script and ask a friend to read the words to you as you relax. Then develop a script for the friend and return the favor. You can have a lot of fun creating scripts and going through the process together, as well as support each other in your goals. Have a hypno-spa day and invite a few friends to get facials and do hypnosis. This is a cool way to make yourselves look good and feel great inside at the same time.

Live Hypnosis with Debra

Join in on my live hypnosis sessions on my teleseminars and radio show if you would like to experience more self-hypnosis by a professional at little or no cost. I also offer prerecorded mp3 downloads for purchase. Sign up for my *Weekly Dating Tips* newsletter at www.letloveinbook.com and receive notifications of my schedule and when a Let Love In workshop is coming to your area. You can experience wonderful results even in a group setting.

How Do You Know whether Hypnosis Is Working?

Some people see an immediate transformation and tangible results right away, while others feel as if nothing has changed. Everyone processes differently, and you have a unique life experience. The amount of work that you have done prior to reading this book often has a significant effect on how quickly you see progress in your daily life. There are no rules, however, because some people who have done no prior personal growth work and had no previous therapy will begin to change immediately when their core beliefs have been transformed.

Typically, the mind makes a shift within thirty to ninety days of consistent self-hypnosis. Avoid tackling too many issues at once. Don't attempt to work on your love life, weight loss, and attracting money all in the same month. Too many different messages can dilute your efforts. I recommend starting with your deepest core issue, and you will find that other surface problems seem to get resolved automatically.

To measure your progress, revisit the Relationship Assessment Questionnaire at the beginning of this book and reassess yourself after thirty days. Or, every few weeks you can ask yourself an uncovering question (from step 2, "Uncover your beliefs," on page 251) that brings up subconscious beliefs to see what shows up. For example, "When I think about having a healthy relationship, I think . . ." You can do this uncovering exercise weekly to gauge your progress. You should notice that the naysayer voice becomes increasingly quiet and empowering thoughts arise more easily.

Pay attention to what is happening in the external world. Are you dating nicer guys? Do you feel more attractive? Do your friends or family notice a change in your attitude? Your outer world is simply feedback for what is going on in the deepest levels of your mind. Everything that happens to you is a direct result of your subconscious thinking. Being conscious of the details of your life can provide illuminating clues to help you discern what parts of your mind are clear and what still needs to be tweaked on the subconscious level so that you can attract your man.

Meditation Practice

Another fantastic way that you can support your work is through meditation. Avoid confusing self-hypnosis with daily meditation. Anything you can do to relax your mind is a good practice, but hypnosis and pure meditation are slightly different. You can enjoy wonderful benefits from adding a regular meditation practice to your daily hypnosis. Hypnosis is a great tool for reconditioning your subconscious mind, and the practice of meditation helps you focus your mind and become more present. Together, they work to help you manage your mind in more powerful ways.

Many people think of meditation as a relaxation exercise or a guided visualization (like self-hypnosis). The pure practice of meditation, however, does not involve relaxation or visualization. The goal is to be fully present with your body, your thoughts, and your spirit.

You can sit in a chair or on a cushion on the floor. Sit up with your back straight (do not lie down). Some practices recommend opening your eyes slightly so that you can remain alert. Simply sit with yourself and pay attention to your breath. When a thought comes to your mind, just let the idea float by without attempting to hold on to it by examining or judging it. Return to your breath if your mind wanders, and gently nudge yourself back to the present moment. Do this for ten to thirty minutes a day. There is no goal except to be aware of yourself and how your mind reacts to being still.

This process sometimes causes people to feel uncomfortable at first. How many times have you sat quietly by yourself without distractions such as listening to the radio, having the TV on, taking a phone call, reading a book, and so on? We are conditioned to be busy and distracted, so meditation helps you become comfortable with doing nothing. You can increase your level of self-acceptance when you allow yourself to sit and be just as you are without judgment.

The biggest misconception about meditation is that you have to shut off your mind. Your mind never shuts off (even while you sleep), so achieving this goal would be an impossible feat. The frustration that certain people feel with meditation comes from their trying to do the impossible. Instead, know that there is no goal except to sit and be with yourself.

Pure meditation practice can help you become more focused in the moment and able to manage the influx of thoughts that constantly bombards you. As you learn to step back and become an observer of your thoughts, you can avoid being caught up in them. Over time, as you sit with yourself, you will witness subtle changes in your pattern of thinking. You will become free of your mental demons and will have access to your inner divine spirit, your true essence.

Embracing the Real You

Who are you . . . really? I hope you are starting to transform the old beliefs and limitations of your previous identity. Beyond all of the rejections, bad dates, self-doubts, and fear, there lies a beautiful, limitless spirit. As you awaken to your real self, you begin to realize the power inside of you. No longer willing to be what others want you to be, you become the creator of your life.

The only barrier between you and your amazing self is your limited belief system. Dragging the past along with you keeps you shackled to it as you repeat the same patterns. Breaking old relationship habits can be challenging because your mind wants so much to keep you the same. You may experience a little discomfort as you step into your power, and that is completely normal. Your mind will try to convince you to retreat, that this growth stuff is too hard and that you are just not strong enough—don't fall for it! This is where your faith steps in to override the default setting in your subconscious and give you the energy to control your thoughts. Keep imagining the result you seek, as if love already has arrived.

As you continue to focus your thinking in the direction of true love, you create a new groove of being. Each day the resistance diminishes until your mind finally succumbs to embracing the real you. You are always in control and can refuse to give away your power to your subconscious mind. Take back the reins and stay in your lane on the expressway toward love.

Some women meet their true loves within thirty days of working with their subconscious blocks, while others may take up to six months or longer. No matter how effective the hypnosis exercises are for you, you still have your will. It may be silly, but some people undertake programs like this just to prove that something does not work. They derive a sad comfort from feeling sorry for themselves that not even the best hypnotist in the world can change.

You are in control of your life. You always have been and always will be. The results will show up in the way that you want them to appear. Some of your inner desires can be counterproductive, and you now have the tools to uncover and transform them. The bottom line is that you make the choice. Your attitude is the most important component of this process.

Being clear on what you want and having every aspect of your mind in alignment with your desire is the initial hurdle to conquer. If you take action to support your goals and have faith that your desires will be realized, this will accelerate the process. It's beneficial to do the following exercise when you need a quick clearing to get in sync with what you want to create. Before you begin the next visualization, write in your journal something specific that you would like to attract into your life. Follow these guidelines:

- Focus on the end result (not on the steps leading up to what you really want; the universe will take care of the details).

- State your intention with clarity (the universe responds literally to your requests, so be careful with your wording).

- Make sure your intention is stated in the positive; the subconscious mind cancels out the negative words and simply picks up on the main idea.

- Make sure your intention is stated in the present tense (as if you already have achieved the result). For example, instead of saying, "I will attract my mate," you should say, "I am attracting my mate."

- Imagine that you have what you desire. Make sure you engage emotion when you are visualizing. Really feel as if your strong will is actually drawing your desires to you.

- Let go of expectations, and wait to see what arrives. Your desires may not show up in the way that you expect. When you set your intention, always hold the idea "If not this, something better."

Have fun with this. Like the genie in Aladdin's lamp, the universe will respond to your request with "Your wish is my command."

SELF-HYPNOSIS

Realize Your Desires

Be sure to read through the entire exercise before you start.

Use your favorite induction and deepener and pick a peaceful place to go in your mind.

Imagine that you are standing in your peaceful place. Take in all of the sights, smells, and sounds. Feel a warm breeze; the sun is shining just right. Become grounded and calm. You can bring in your "good feeling" if you like.

Even though your eyes are closed, imagine a beautiful scroll appearing in front of you and a pen floating next to it. Notice at the top of the scroll the words "My Desires." You realize that this is the special place in your mind where you set your intentions for manifestation. This may be the first time you have been here or that you knew you had the power to create anything in your life that you desire. Now you are here and are filled with a sense of calm and peace, knowing that you are in control. You have unlimited resources.

Move the pen with your mind and write your intention across the scroll. Remember to make your desire positive, clear, and in the present tense.

(Pause)

Now that you have written your intention, allow the scroll to roll up and turn into a beautiful beam of light rising higher and higher to the greater reaches of the universe so that your intention can be created in your life.

(Optional: You can visualize your spirit guides, angels, or fairies taking the scroll or imagine that you are sending it up to God to fulfill.)

Now you must clear away all blocks within your subconscious mind that would keep your dreams from becoming reality. Find in your peaceful place a beautiful waterfall of light. Stand under the waterfall and imagine a wonderful soft golden light flowing in through the top of your head, down your body, and out through your feet. Imagine this light melting away any tension or doubts that you have in receiving your intention. If you like, you may think of the doubts and fears as a dark cloud leaving you while you cleanse your mind and body in the wonderful golden waterfall of light. Feel your body becoming lighter and lighter and lighter. Find yourself losing all sense of your physical body as you go deeper and deeper into a trance. Release any blocks to your desires through this cleansing exercise.

(Pause)

Now, if your subconscious mind hasn't released all of the blocks, direct your inner mind to find those counter-intentions and release them right now. Your subconscious mind is very intelligent and knows how to do this powerfully and effectively.

(Short pause)

You will see a beautiful doorway in the garden that is labeled, "My Future." Open the door and step into the future, where you experience your desire being fulfilled right now. Fill in all of the details. Remember to evoke the emotion of what it feels like to actually possess what you wrote down as your intention. Take a few minutes to really engage all of your senses and bring that result into your consciousness.

(Pause)

Now come back through the door into your special place. Remember that you can imagine your future anytime by simply going there in your mind. Know that you have done everything right and that the universe is working toward bringing your intention to you right now. Deep within your heart space, imagine that a beautiful ball of light appears, which represents your unwavering faith. Allow that light to grow brighter and to surround you, enfolding you in a wonderful certainty that your desires are being realized. This light surrounds and protects you from outside influences that may try to destroy your faith. You remain safe within your bubble of light, which works deep within your subconscious mind to continue to clear away any thoughts that are not aligned with your goal.

Let go of expectations and allow the universe to take care of the details regarding how and when you will reach your goal. Pay attention to your intuition, as it guides you to certain places or to do specific things that may help you achieve your desire. You are present and focused when listening to your inner guidance. Relax and let go, relax and trust, relax and believe that you are getting everything you desire. You are a powerful spiritual being; you are unlimited. You have the power to create your life. You are becoming more powerful each and every day. You are in sync with the laws of life. Your energy vibration is becoming clearer so that you can succeed at things more easily than ever before. Each day in every way, you feel better and better and better.

All of these ideas have made a permanent impression on your subconscious mind. You will see these ideas realized in greater and more powerful ways than you can imagine. Count up to five and open your eyes.

After completing the exercise, feel free to record your desires in your journal and date the entry. Watch your visions unfold, and keep a record of how they appear in your life. Notice what is working for you, and fine-tune your process as needed. If something does not materialize, change the wording of your intention or use another exercise in this book to address and clear away the blockage.

When You Meet "Him"

He has finally arrived in your life! Hurrah! After you date for a while, you begin to feel that he is the one for you. What next? Here are some quick tips to keep you on track.

- *Nothing has changed.* Avoid defining yourself as successful because you now have reached your goal and met your man. You are still the same wonderful person that you were when you were single. You were always good enough and will not lose anything if the relationship doesn't work out. Holding this idea in your mind will keep the attraction flowing between the two of you. He did not save you; you saved yourself.

- *Feeling uncomfortable is normal.* You have been unfamiliar with true love, so it makes sense that you feel a little nervous and uncertain. Remember that you can dictate the pace of the relationship and you don't have to open up completely all at once. Take your time and get your subconscious mind used to the experience of being loved and adored. Soon enough, your subconscious mind will not accept anything less than wonderful.

- *Focus on his positive traits*. Instead of picking the poor guy apart to look for flaws and reasons not to be with him, focus on what you like about him. What you see in him, you see in yourself. He will subconsciously feel good around you and will take notice of your wonderful traits as well.

- *Don't worry about making mistakes*. The right man for you will love you for all of your qualities. Don't be on guard, fearful that you will make the wrong move and scare him away. If he gets freaked out by who you are, he was not your guy in the first place. Keep your focus on your best self, and that is what he will see as well if he is worthy of you. Don't stress about following others' dating rules. My friend Lori says, "When he's the right one, you can make all the mistakes in the world and he'll still love you." Sound advice.

- *Only fools rush in*. Take one step at a time, and don't rush into being a couple, engaged and planning the wedding . . . just yet. Many single women rationalize that they need to know sooner rather than later whether their guy is commitment material. These single women feel as if they have wasted enough time on the wrong guys. You may be anxious to solidify your bond. Why not? You have waited long enough. The need to rush into commitment is motivated by the part of you that is afraid of losing him. But you don't have to put a vise grip on someone to make him to stay. If you think you do, then you need to read this book again to figure out what you missed.

- *New stuff comes up*. You may have thought you were done with working on personal growth now that you have found your man. Not quite. As you become closer to him, new issues will arise that you have not addressed yet. Because being in a healthy relationship may be new to you, you probably have no idea what else could be lurking in your subconscious mind. Look at this process as fun. You have all of the tools you need, and you can use the exercises in this book to work on any other blockages to love that an intimate relationship with your dream man exposes.

Be patient with yourself and compassionate about your process. Your guy loves you, regardless of those little quirks.

When your meet your true love, you will probably know it right away. He will be so different from your past loves, but somehow so familiar, as if you've known him forever. Everyone has a unique experience of finally finding that special someone. On our second date my partner, Roberto, gave me this poem he had written. Before hypnosis, I had always run away in fear when a man showed so much interest in me. Yet now I knew that my deep mind had changed because I allowed Roberto into my heart.

All my work, all my study now seems like dust and ashes
since you offered me your delicate hands across the table.
A woman like you, earthy but ethereal, is a jewel of
existence.
Ordinary men cannot perceive—
but I, a wandering pilgrim
wounded in a thousand battles of the soul,
can feel the depths of your subtle spirit,
the secret chamber of your mystic heart.

Eliud R. Maldonado, PhD

Conclusion: You Are Already Perfect

Once the realization is accepted that even between the closest human beings infinite distances continue, a wonderful living side by side can grow, if they succeed in loving the distance between them which makes it possible for each to see the other whole against the sky.

—Rainer Maria Rilke

Keep the faith, whether the process of finding your true love takes one month, six months, or longer. Everyone has a unique route to his or her destiny. Just because that special someone has not appeared yet, it doesn't mean that all is lost. The techniques in this book have changed you in profound ways that you may not realize. Keep visualizing, believing, and following your heart. No matter what has happened up until now, today could be the day that you meet the love of your life.

Wherever you are in your search for love, remember that you are already perfect. There is nothing to change, improve on, or fix . . . *except your false perceptions.* The truth is that you are lovable, amazing, wonderful, and absolutely worthy of love. You may now come to understand that you had love within you all along. Your perfect relationship has always been nearby, simply waiting for you to let love in.

Index